Developing Youth Soccer Players

Horst Wein

Human Kinetics

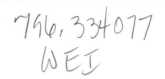
Library of Congress Cataloging-in-Publication Data

Wein, Horst.
    Developing youth soccer players / Horst Wein.
        p.   cm.
    Includes bibliographical references.
    ISBN 0-7360-0354-1
        1. Soccer for children--Coaching.   2. Soccer for children--Training.   I. Title.
GV943.8.W45   2000
796.334'07'7--dc21   00-027310

ISBN: 0-7360-0354-1

This book is a revised edition of *L'insegnamento programmato nel calcio*, published in 1988 by Edizioni Mediterrannee and *Fútbol a la medida del niño*, published in 1997 by Real Federación Española de Fútbol.

Acquisitions Editor: Jeff Riley; **Developmental Editor**: Laura Hambly; **Assistant Editor**: Stephan Seyfert; **Copyeditor**: Anne Heiles; **Proofreader**: Kathy Bennett; **Permission Manager**: Cheri Banks; **Graphic Designer**: Nancy Rasmus; **Graphic Artist**: Sandra Meier; **Photo Editor**: Clark Brooks; **Cover Designer**: Jack W. Davis; **Photographer (cover)**: © Horst Wein/photo by Adolfo Sebastiano; **Photographer (interior)**: Tom Roberts unless otherwise noted; photos on pages v, 8, 16, 29, 75, 79, 121, 123, 151, 183, 209, and 211 by Adolfo Sebastiano/© Horst Wein; **Illustrator**: Mic Greenberg; drawings by Benjamin Echevarren/© Horst Wein

Human Kinetics books are available at special discounts for bulk purchase. Special editions or book excerpts can also be created to specification. For details, contact the Special Sales Manager at Human Kinetics.

Printed in Hong Kong

10   9   8   7   6   5   4   3   2   1

Human Kinetics
Web site: **http://www.humankinetics.com/**

United States: Human Kinetics
P.O. Box 5076, Champaign, IL 61825-5076
800-747-4457
e-mail: humank@hkusa.com

Canada: Human Kinetics
475 Devonshire Road Unit 100, Windsor, ON N8Y 2L5
800-465-7301 (in Canada only)
e-mail: humank@hkcanada.com

Europe: Human Kinetics
P.O. Box IW14, Leeds LS16 6TR, United Kingdom
+44 (0)113-278 1708
e-mail: humank@hkeurope.com

Australia: Human Kinetics
57A Price Avenue, Lower Mitcham, South Australia 5062
(08) 82771555
e-mail: liahka@senet.com.au

New Zealand: Human Kinetics
P.O. Box 105-231, Auckland Central
09-309-1890
e-mail: humank@hknewz.com

Acknowledgments must go to many players,
coaches, and sport scientists
of all levels and different sports
who have inspired me
to extend and deepen my soccer knowledge,
thus providing me with the raw material
for this manual.

Contents

Foreword

It's a great satisfaction for me to learn that Horst Wein's Soccer Development Model, which has been so well accepted in Spain and other countries, is now published in this English-language edition. *Developing Youth Soccer Players* opens the door for a multitude of coaches and children, highly enthusiastic about soccer, to be exposed to his unique philosophy and highly successful method of teaching.

The valuable experience he shares in this book will serve coaches as both a teaching and learning model. Excellent drawings and photos clearly illustrate the games in his program and reflect the art of teaching young soccer players.

Throughout this book, Horst Wein describes a methodology of teaching soccer that never limits a child's entertainment or creativity, but rather allows children to enjoy every second of the learning process. The pleasure of playing soccer should never be restricted by severe rules.

Young players are the cornerstone of soccer. They are, and always will be, the future of the sport. Much more important than winning games is the acquisition of those values inherent in soccer—fair play, the urge to do better, and the sportive spirit. Education, therefore, runs parallel to the technical instruction. This is how soccer proves its enormous social dimension.

In this way, we welcome the well-known slogan of FIFA President Joseph Blattner, "Soccer for everybody, everybody for soccer." We applaud as well his initiative to start the "Goal Project," which, during the coming years, will propel a series of activities toward developing soccer play and education among children.

I am happy to see the largest soccer organization in the world, FIFA, and also the Real Federación Española de Fútbol promoting the messages in Horst Wein's *Developing Youth Soccer Players*. Through this approach, they foster the aim to make our sport even more popular and thus to ensure its future.

Angel Maria Villar

President, Real Federación Española de Fútbol
Football Committee Chairman, Fédération Internationale de Football Associations
(FIFA)

Preface

All too often, children are introduced to complex sports activities for which they are not yet physically and mentally ready. Expecting a child to comprehend and respond to the complex situations in the full 11-on-11 soccer game format will only beget frustration and feelings of failure. *Developing Youth Soccer Players* introduces coaches to a training program that takes into account each young player's current physical and mental development. The program promotes the gradual development of correct technical, tactical, and physical capacities of soccer players ages 7 to 14.

This book features the *Soccer Development Model*, an innovative system of coaching in which stimulation is specific to each age group's cognitive capacities and physical abilities. Most books for youth soccer coaching present general instruction and drills to be applied to all children who participate, regardless of their age. In this book, however, stimulation fitted to the appropriate development stage replaces generalized instruction.

This model is essentially a recipe for coaching soccer. It gives you the necessary ingredients of the game and the proportions in which these ingredients have to be mixed to achieve enjoyable and effective training sessions. Most importantly, it explains what skills are best taught during each stage of the evolution of young soccer players. All of the research has been done; you can simply apply it to your coaching program.

Developing Youth Soccer Players is divided into eight chapters. Chapter 1 explains the developmental characteristics of children and describes how most current coaching practices actually work against players' developing minds and bodies. According to these practices, children are coached the same ways as adults, even though the adult game is much too complex for a child's mental and motor abilities. The solution to this problem is provided in chapter 2, which explains the different levels of the developmental model, including how and why it was created. Making use of the Soccer Development Model in schools and clubs reduces the acquisition of incorrect habits that limit the performance of players at the senior level. These incorrect habits result directly from the way players have been taught and have competed at lower levels.

Chapter 3 contains basic games and exercises that make up the first level of the Soccer Development Model. You'll learn games and exercises to teach your young players the fundamentals, such as juggling and balancing the ball; dribbling; passing, receiving, and shooting; and tackling. Level 1 also contains simplified competitions—the soccer decathlon and 2-on-2 triathlon—for players ages 7 and up.

Chapter 4 introduces you to the second level in the Soccer Development Model. Using a number of simplified game situations, players learn to respond to the cognitive and physical demands of the game. The simplified game preserves the contextual nature of the full game without placing too great a technical demand on players in these early stages. *Learning to understand the complex game of soccer can be best achieved through the practice of a logical progression of simplified games, with a gradual increase in the number of players on the teams.* Level 2 also contains competitions tailored to this age group—mini-soccer 3 on 3, the Mini-Soccer Pentathlon, and the 3-on-3 triathlon.

Chapters 5 and 6 progress to Level 3, which pertains to players ages 10 years and up. You'll learn additional simplified games and competitions that gradually increase in complexity from the games in Level 2. Level 3 also contains a program for developing young goalkeepers. It describes the most important qualities necessary to be a goalkeeper, and it offers exercises to enhance and develop these skills.

Chapter 7 gives you the tools for training players ages 12 years and up. This chapter presents a detailed description of Level 4 in the Soccer Development Model. It includes more simplified games that closely link to the appropriate level of competition, 8-on-8 soccer—considered an ideal bridge for leading young athletes to the full soccer game. Game-oriented practice, as you find here, stimulates participants more than traditional instruction and training sessions, in which the contents are isolated from the competition.

The games and drills in chapters 3 through 7 are also complemented by a superior collection of more than 200 full-color illustrations that help put the concepts in motion. The games and exercises are divided according to age and ability level.

Because of the international popularity of soccer, metric measurements are provided throughout the text. The equivalent imperial measurements can easily be found by referring to the chart located in the back of the book.

Chapter 8 emphasizes the only way to develop healthy, happy, and talented soccer players is to tailor coaching instruction to follow young soccer players' natural development. To rush this development is to hinder their healthful formation and future performance.

It is time for all coaches, from novices to the experienced, to revise their ways of coaching and tailor their training sessions and competitions to the children they are teaching. *Developing Youth Soccer Players* is the tool you need to develop a successful soccer program with satisfied young players.

PART I
A New Philosophy of Coaching Soccer

Whether young players choose soccer as a lifelong sport is determined to a high degree by the content of the training program, the expertise and experience of the coaches, the social life in the club or school, and the structure of the formative competitions. The art of developing effective training and competitive programs for children lies in knowing which kind of practice and competition the player is ready for at any given stage of his or her physical and mental development. *Children will only learn quickly, effectively, and thoroughly when the demands of the training sessions or competitions they participate in match their intellectual, psychological, and motor skills.*

The concept of readiness (the disposition of a certain degree of maturity) is a prerequisite for any activity and one that should be applied in all aspects of teaching and learning. Before a child is admitted to school, teachers ask themselves whether the child is ready or mature enough to attend school or whether he or she is prepared to benefit from the teaching process. Teachers determine if the child can successfully meet the challenges of the first school year or if it would be better to let the child mature for one more year with activities that better match his or her mental and physical condition.

The question of maturity is also important in the matter of motor learning. Regardless of the action, adults must determine the age at which there are certain likelihoods that the child can achieve an objective. Before teaching a child to ride a bike, for example, you must first ask when children generally acquire the capacity to maintain balance on only two wheels. Experience has shown us that any attempt to teach the skill before the child is ready (before about four years of age) will fail because nature has not yet provided the means of coordination and balance.

The concept of readiness must also be applied to children's sports activities. Coaches should ask, "At what age is a child ready to successfully face the demands of an adult competition?" If officials were aware of the concept of readiness, children under the age of 14 in our various sport clubs would never have been subjected to testing themselves in competitions for which they were not yet qualified, prepared, or simply ready. Children must be exposed to a gradual stimulation in training and to a series of progressive competitions that, over the years, allows them to grow step by step into the adult game. The art of teaching lies largely in knowing for what activity (a technical move, a tactical behavior, or a complex competition) the player is prepared for at a particular stage of physical and mental development.

Unfortunately, it is the force of habit that constitutes the greatest obstacle to progress in youth soccer. Traditional methods are often followed blindly—adherents not giving sufficient thought to the training's consequences or the competition's structure. To achieve better results, coaches, administrations, and federations must first review the structure and organization of their youth soccer programs. The complicated adult game has to be simplified; a logical progression of competitions must be created, designed with gradual increasing demands that adapt perfectly to the mental and physical capacities of individual children. Youngsters should be presented with only those exercises, games, and challenges that suit their current abilities, interests, and expectations. *The training programs and competitions for children should be like their shoes: they should fit perfectly and feel comfortable.*

If we are to improve the development of young players, it is crucial that we recognize past mistakes. Awareness of errors is the first step toward more effective training and learning methods.

The Natural Development of Young Players

"Nature decrees that children should be children before they become adults. If we try to alter this natural order, we will reach adulthood prematurely but with neither substance nor strength."

Jean J. Rousseau

All things in nature have a gestation period and must go through their proper stages to be formed. Each human being has to pass through different stages of development before finally reaching maturity. Nature does not take shortcuts; there is a natural, unhurried order to it all.

Coaches, players, parents, and administrators should copy the wisdom of nature. Being impatient and hurrying the development of young soccer players in the teaching and learning processes frequently results in poor performances among older players who had shown promise when they were younger. What coaches need is a training plan or model they can perfectly tailor to fit their players' varying cognitive and motor abilities.

To work with the developing mind and body of individuals, all youth soccer competitions and training programs must respect the laws of nature and take into account the actual mental and physical condition of their young participants. As children mature, the games in which they compete should gradually become more difficult and complex. *In a well-structured scheme, young soccer players grow at the same rate as their competitions grow in complexity and difficulty.*

Current Coaching Practices

Most players, no matter their nationality, don't know how to tap into or make use of their potential. Sadly, the best coaches do not work at the grass roots level because coaching young soccer players rarely reaps them any economic gain. Coaches with greater knowledge and experience are attracted instead to senior teams that can afford to provide them higher salaries.

This failure to attract well-qualified coaches means that young players in schools and clubs are exposed to poor quality and tedious instruction. In most cases, children are coached in the same way that adults are instructed, without taking into account the natural order or progressive development of the young player through time. The makeshift or haphazard schemes that most coaches adopt do not solve the delicate problem of assuring young players quality coaching. Moreover, coaching youth at the initial stages is too important for the future development of the players to allow coaches to hastily assemble idiosyncratic methods of training.

Introducing Complex Activities Too Soon

One problem with most methods of training and competition is that they employ complex games and playing situations before children are ready for them. Even soccer players competing at the club level generally fail one out of three plays, so we must admit that soccer is a complicated game. Research has shown, generally speaking, that the younger the player, the higher the percentage of failure in competition. A low success rate (fewer than 50 percent of successful actions) is observed when beginners between 8 and 9 years of age compete with only seven players on a team (7 on 7). Players face countless difficulties and complex problems even in a game played with this pared-down team. In competition with 11 players on a team, as still happens in many parts of the world, one team lost the possession of the ball four to six times in just one minute's play!

Young players should not be blamed for incurring this high percentage of unsuccessful actions. We must realize that all children fail frequently, not only in soccer but also in other physical and mental activities, if they are not brought to the task gradually and progressively. In today's training and competition, children are asked to face game situations that are simply beyond their limits or scope at that particular stage of their psychomotor development. Subjecting children to complex activities before they're ready only reinforces failure and frustration. When individuals experience frequent failure, they not only lose interest and self-esteem but may also come to feel incapable of facing situations that, in fact, are far too difficult and complex for them at the time. Stress and dropping out may result.

Demanding Too Much of Young Players

Teaching or learning soccer, as well as competing in it, the traditional way does not sufficiently stimulate the bodies and minds of young players, and much of their talent is left undiscovered. Playing the ball for a maximum of 90 seconds in a full match or being active for fewer than 15 minutes of a 90-minute training session doesn't allow players to develop their full potential. Yet players are still expected and pressured to perform at a high level. This puts an ever-increasing demand on the youngsters' physical and mental abilities and capacities.

Using Inefficient Coaching Methods

Consider this: many children study a foreign language over the course of eight years in school. If the youth then travel to a country where their mother language is not spoken, however, they are frequently unable to apply the knowledge they have acquired in almost a thousand hours of teaching and learning. Likewise, most recently-graduated physical education teachers, after studying four years of different sport sciences in a physical education department of a university, still cannot resolve the majority of the innumerable problems they encounter during their first physical education lessons. This is caused by insufficient practical applications of their studies and insufficient experience—in addition to applying methods that are already out of date. The knowledge gained at universities or in national training centers has helped few coaches to confront the challenges of their profession with success.

To be up to date and make use of the new information (most of which tends to repeat itself about every two decades), physical education teachers (and especially those who coach future teachers) should actualize and constantly augment their knowledge and capacities to help their students learn the latest innovations of their specialization.

The tragedy of coaching young players focuses on the fact that many coaches may know a lot about the game, but they don't know their young pupils.

The major obstacle for the progress of coaching in soccer is the strength of ease and comfort. Because of their own inertia or sluggishness, *coaches tend to continue with old habits rather than continually rethinking what has to be done and how.* All too often information is used and exercises and formative programs are applied that have already lost their validity. Many have not even noticed that the information they obtained years before has diminished in value.

Few coaches look beyond their specialty and combine, mix, or synthesize the knowledge from diverse but related sports sciences with the teaching and learning process. Consequently, the majority of players and coaches must continue learning from accidents, mistakes, and trials rather than from the instruction received.

Before teaching a specific sport like soccer, coaches should fully understand how a child, adolescent, or adult learns best and analyze the mechanisms that intervene and influence learning in each of the evolutionary stages of the student. As the young soccer player grows and develops, a great variety of physiological, cognitive, and social-emotional changes occur that directly affect the acquisition of coordination and conditional, as well as mental, capacities.

Time for a Change!

In these days of increasingly sedentary and easy living habits, relatively few minutes of the day are reserved for physical stimuli or allowing children to use their creativity, imagination, and initiative. Under these conditions, the entire tradition of coaching must be rethought and carefully revised to give players a more "hands on" role in their own education.

Promoting Active Participation

Rather than adhering to current soccer programs that concentrate on the execution of different skills, the modern coach should teach pupils to understand all aspects of the game. Too much drill will kill the young players' innate potential! Over time, coaches should carefully and progressively develop important capacities, including perception, analysis of game situations, and correct decision making under stressful conditions.

Yet a coach cannot foster these qualities through verbal instruction alone. When coaches continually use verbal instruction, they become the main actors in the coaching theater, thereby curtailing or even killing the active participation of the players. Usurping the active role is detrimental to the players' effective learning. By involving the players, on the other hand, a coach obliges them to think, to collect information, to organize the collected information and come to conclusions, to evaluate and judge, to imagine, invent, and create new moves or combinations.

"Youth prefer to be stimulated instead of being instructed."

Johann Wolfgang von Goethe

In *Coaching of Performance* John Whitmore (1997) wrote that a pupil only remembers 19 percent of what the teacher taught him or her some three months ago through instructing or telling, whereas he or she can recall 32 percent of what was demonstrated and explained. Yet in cases where pupils were given the opportunity to generate the information on their own, but with the help of a teacher, fully 65 percent of the information was memorized.

That is why soccer players should be allowed to actively participate in the coaching and learning process: to develop as complete athletes who eventually become independent from the frequent instruction of coaches. *Learning takes place best when the coach is able to transfer decisions to the pupils.*

Allowing Children More Control

Creativity can be considered one of a human being's most elevated mental activities. Unfortunately, few coaches know how to stimulate this ability in their players. The

Ten Rules for Learning Efficiency

1. Acquire good habits. Bad habits double the amount of work for the coach because he or she must first suppress the incorrect habit and then teach the student to react correctly to the same stimulus. Just as one can learn to speak a language well or poorly, one can also acquire good or bad habits and behaviors in soccer.

2. Confront players with problems that are within their capabilities—and also with slightly more complex and difficult activities that, after a certain number of trials, can be mastered without help from the coach. A feeling of capability and success generally nourishes and stimulates learning. When players are aware of their capability and receive some kind of reward for their success, learning will be fun and players will be encouraged to progress even further.

3. Help players learn to recognize the result of every play immediately after the action is over. Players who are conscious of the results of their play in a given game situation will be capable of later reproducing or suppressing the vivid experience in a similar game situation.

4. Teach new aspects of the game within the parameters of ones that are already known. People tend to learn more quickly when they already partially know the abilities and capacities that the coach is trying to develop.

5. Practice the individual elements of a situation to connect the stimulus and response. The first phase of learning is to recognize a game situation that is composed of various elements. To better recognize a situation, it's important to practice it many times. Apart from facilitating recognition of a situation, the repetitions tend to strengthen the connection between the stimuli and the correct answer.

6. Review and repeat material frequently. Because the loss of an ability or capacity starts right after the first practice, repetition is vital to learning. A few repetitions succeed in activating only short-term memory. Transferring information to long-term memory requires repetitions of the same task, in the event these tasks will be varied by the coach on more than two occasions, in *more than* two training sessions.

7. Vary the exercises and games. Without varying the content of a practice, you risk boring players. To avoid monotony, loss of concentration, and lack of motivation in the players—all enemies of learning—the coach must ensure variety in the session.

8. Mix up the flow of content. The more similar the content of different parts of a training session, the higher the interference becomes between them. This is because the last thing learned is frequently superimposed on what was previously learned. Remaining on the same theme or method of presentation of the content for even 15 to 20 minutes can lower players' concentration and interest.

9. Motivate your pupils and players, be it through praise or a choice of activities that interests them. Motivation supports learning.

10. Stimulate both the body and the whole mind. Bulgarian scientist Georgi Losanow discovered a "super learning" method in the 1970s: maximum learning occurs when teachers use an activity to stimulate both the left and right hemispheres of the brain (Ostrander et al. 1979). Soccer's traditional teaching methods often fail to adequately stimulate the right hemisphere of the brain, which harbors the creative capacities, intuition, and space and time orientation. Each training session should stimulate the body as well as both hemispheres of the brain.

Presenting players with problems they solve on their own results in better decisions during games.

teaching styles and rigid methods seen on most soccer fields tend to strangulate more than stimulate the players' capacity of fantasy, creativity, and innovation.

During training, instead of giving young children sufficient opportunities to cultivate their innate potential, coaches tend to dominate everything, fearful of losing control of the situation by giving up any control to the players. *A coach's objective should be to make the others think,* instead of thinking for them.

Expert coaches with a wealth of technical knowledge often have a hard time withholding their expertise. They are used to giving away their knowledge through many instructions about what, when, and how to do the task, without being aware that coaching this way will limit their pupils' formation. Giving the players solutions to "remember" should be replaced by presenting them with tailor-made problems that they have to *resolve on their own.*

Stimulating Players' Minds

To develop players' active involvement in the training and learning process, coaches must master the skill of posing questions. The most effective questions are open ones that require descriptive answers. In contrast, closed questions with "yes" or "no" answers shut the door on the exploration of further detail. That is why coaches should concentrate on open questions, ones that begin with words that seek to quantify or gather facts: *what, when, how much,* or *how many.*

Through systematic questioning by the coach the pupils are self-generating the information. Thanks to intelligent questions, many players become aware of problems they have never noticed before. Facing them, players have to think, examine, judge, and evaluate until they find solutions to the problems presented by the coach. On the contrary, when a coach instructs or just tells players what to do in certain moments or situations of the game, he or she does not stimulate any of these active mental processes.

Once soccer coaches have been convinced of the need to modify the traditional way of teaching their players, they soon discover that the process of understanding and learning soccer will shift increasingly to self-teaching.

Meeting Young People's Needs

The key to developing successful youth soccer players is in understanding and meeting the needs of young players, rather than subjecting them to boring exercises or a game designed for adults. These are some basic, yet important, needs children have that coaches should always keep in mind.

➤ **Need for security.** During training, children need a familiar and intimate atmosphere that gives them security and confidence. It's not recommended to frequently change the training site nor the coach or educator. Returning to games that are already familiar (but meeting variations of them) is welcomed by the kids so long as the contents of the training sessions link with something they already know. The children demand stable relations.

On a related note, training should always take place in a safe environment, and specific rules should be applied to ensure safety and avoid any dangerous situations.

➤ **Need for new experiences.** Nothing can be understood completely as long as it has not been experienced. Coaches should allow the children to experiment with tasks. Children need to discover on their own everything that surrounds them. Kids should be stimulated with games and activities that are within their physical and mental capacities. This method of coaching allows them to develop their abilities and capacities step by step through their own discovery.

➤ **Need to be acknowledged.** Children get highly motivated when tribute is paid to their efforts in mastering a skill or problem. Through praise they are encouraged to try even harder. To children younger than 12 years old, the teacher, coach, or parent is like a mirror in which they see their capacity or incapacity. That is why educators and parents have to learn to be positive, to praise the children frequently and keep critical comments to a minimum.

➤ **Need to show responsibility.** Children prefer to do things on their own without depending too much on adults. They like to reach independence as quickly as possible. The coaching methods and behavior of the educator should consider this need, making sure that the children are frequently allowed to find their own solutions to problems the coach presents. The educator should interfere only when the problems can't be solved by the pupils.

Youngsters can also perform the tasks of putting down or collecting cones, modifying the rules of a practice game, or choosing players for demonstrations or certain activities. Their need to demonstrate responsibility can also be stimulated in each training session by allowing them 10 minutes in which to freely choose what to practice, how to do it, and where and with whom to execute a determined skill or game.

Coaches who are reluctant to give up some of the responsibility to the children must realize that learning also takes place out of their presence. In any team game, children organize their play in its logical fashion even if an adult is not available to guide them. First they make sure that the teams are even. They want competition. They want the game to be fair and challenging, thus forcing them to play to their full potential. Second, kids don't need referees. The players take care of the rules themselves, modifying them according to conditions and the environment: no offside, more players, bigger field, and so forth. Third, teams are often composed of players of different ages. The younger players learn from the older ones, who, at the same time, are challenged by the younger players. This is how good teams are built at the senior level as well.

➤ **Need to play.** Playing games is as vital for children as sleep. Playing is necessary for the health of their bodies and minds. As children learn by playing, *the central part of each training session should be the practice and understanding of simplified games.* The art of coaching is to always adapt it to the children's ability and capacity level—and not vice versa. Playing games stimulates communication and decision making. Playing soccer without thinking is like shooting without aiming.

➤ **Need to socialize.** Children instinctively look for communication with others. The older they are, the more they need company of a similar age. They love to be associated with a group and to identify themselves with a group or team with the aim to achieve common objectives.

➤ **Need to move.** Nature wants her children to be active. Youngsters have no patience to wait in queues for their turn. Rules of the adult games must be modified to allow children to play the ball more often. Games with few players assure active participation.

The adult game should be modified to assure active participation among young players.

➤ **Need to live in the present.** Generally spoken, neither the past nor the future interests children very much. Their sense of time is completely different than that of adults. Children live intensely in the present moment without bothering about tomorrow or yesterday, which they deem to be far away.

➤ **Need for variety.** Children crave variety, which results in less boredom and fatigue. A great variety of stimulants is fundamental to maintaining their attention level. Unless you frequently vary the method of presentation and the contents, their attention deviates. Educators also have to vary the intensity of the exercises and games.

➤ **Need to be understood by adults.** Children seem to live in a different world. They have different problems, they learn differently, and they don't think as logically as adults do. Their ideas, thoughts, or reasoning often lack coherence. Their emotional constancy depends in a high degree on their speed of biological growth. In general, kids don't know how to use their energy well and therefore tire easily. They behave exactly the way they feel. For all these reasons, adults who live and work with children should know how to stimulate and guide them in their search for personality and identity.

Eliminating Anxiety

In a study conducted by Pierce and Stratton (1981), 453 youth sport participants were asked to identify the worries that bothered them so much that they might not play in the future. Most of these children indicated that not playing well (63.3 percent) and making a mistake (62.5 percent) were the major stressors when playing sports. Related to these anxieties, 44.2 percent stated that their worries prevented them from playing their best and 23.6 percent suggested that the anxiety might prevent them from playing in the future.

We all know that one main stress factor for children in a competition is the strong desire of their parents and coaches to see them winning. Pressured by the adults, the young players perceive anxiety before, during, and even after the game, instead of competing mainly to have fun with friends.

Administrators, teachers, parents, and other adults tend to evaluate children's abilities and capacities unrealistically high, forcing them to participate in competitions in which the young players will not do well. In turn, the unrealistic expectations cause the youngsters to view themselves as failures, destroying their motivation and self-esteem. But *self-esteem is the life force of the personality,* and if that is suppressed or diminished, so is the person! As a result, children perceive that they will not be able to adequately respond to the performance demands of the difficult and complex competition for which they are not yet ready, one that was originally designed for adults a century ago.

You can help a player a lot by correcting him, but even more by encouraging him.

Already before the game, children are aware of the difficulty of the task (precompetition anxiety). During the game, the young players demonstrate even greater arousal levels when they experience their limitations through making more mistakes than successful moves. Even after the completion of the game, the stress level remains if the completed performance is considered inadequate.

Being more specific, the premature introduction of the 11-on-11 game for prepubescent children causes excessive stress, which then results in negative self-perception. This poor self-image severely hinders the learning process and motivation of the young players.

Young children learn most efficiently in nonstressful environments (Wilson 1984). Prepubescent children have to be exposed in each stage of evolution to a tailor-made competition that assures they perceive their own competence while playing a game.

Recognizing the deficiencies in current practices is the first step to a more effective way of coaching soccer. When children's stages of development are not considered in designing a training program, a gap forms between what the soccer program provides them and what the children need in order to learn. It is time to challenge current coaching practices and stop subjecting children to exercises and games that are too complex to match their mental and physical development. By tailoring the game of soccer to fit the bodies and minds of young players, coaches develop successful soccer programs and happy, talented young players.

Bill of Rights for Young Soccer Players

1. The right to enjoyment both in practice and in competition, with a wide variety of activities that promote fun and easy learning.
2. The right to play as a child and not be treated like an adult, either on or off the playing field.
3. The right to participate in competitions with simplified rules, adapted to their level of ability and capacity in each stage of their evolution.
4. The right to play in conditions of greatest possible safety.
5. The right to participate in all aspects of the game.
6. The right to be trained by experienced and specially prepared coaches and educators.
7. The right to gain experience by resolving most of the problems that arise during the practice.
8. The right to be treated with dignity by the coach, their teammates, and by their opponents.
9. The right to play with children of their own age with similar chances of winning.
10. The right not to become a champion.

A Successful Approach to Coaching Soccer

Planning the development of young players is like preparing for a journey. It's advisable to have a map (plan or model) to avoid getting lost and wasting time and energy.

An effective approach for coaching young players has at last been developed. In this approach, called the "Soccer Development Model," the process has been perfectly adapted to the mental and physical levels of children from different age groups. The model, which all teachers and coaches can follow, could well replace the makeshift training and competitions that have proved ineffective in the past.

The Soccer Development Model is a complete and effective training program that has dramatically influenced the way youngsters in more than 20 countries in Europe, Asia, and South America experience the game of soccer. The model exposes children gradually to the difficulty and complexity of the game. However, far from being a rigid model or training plan, it allows coaches to choose from a proposed menu whatever corresponds to their tastes or coaching styles. Instead of instructing coaches, the Soccer Development Model stimulates them, enabling them to find the best mix of activities for their particular group of players.

The Soccer Development Model

Before applying the model to developing a plan for your young soccer players, let's outline just how the model was created and exactly what it consists of.

Creating the Model

The Soccer Development Model takes into account everything that is known regarding a child's progressive development. It not only respects the laws of nature but also meets the expectations of the young players.

Just as children have basic needs that should be satisfied in designing a soccer program, they also have certain expectations. When children play soccer, they are primarily interested in four things: action, personal involvement in the action, close scores, and opportunities to reaffirm relationships with friends.

Because each of these factors is so important to the well-being of the children, all four were clearly in mind when designing the training and competitive programs in the Soccer Development Model. Numerous changes were made to more traditional training and competitive programs in order to please the children:

➤ The rules of many traditional exercises or games were simplified or modified to increase activity. We know that whenever children create their own games, they devote a good deal of effort to setting up rules that foster action. Most of the activity during their games occurs around the scoring area, and scores are so frequent that everybody scores at least once.

➤ Many exercises and games were designed specifically to increase the personal involvement of all players, allowing them to be in the center of action frequently and therefore feel important.

➤ Changes in game rules and scoring methods helped keep game scores close and heightened challenges. In training, teams are often constructed or modified to keep game scores close enough to make the activity both interesting and challenging, even if outstanding players must accept handicaps.

➤ The organization of teams and practices was changed so that friends have opportunities to play together in a variety of ways.

Children have four phases of motor development (Gallahue 1973), and the design of the Soccer Development Model takes these into consideration. These four phases are

1. reflex movements—from birth until about eight months,
2. rudimentary movements—from the end of the first year of life until the end of the second,
3. fundamental movements—from the second year until about the sixth, and
4. specific or sport movements—from the sixth or seventh year onward.

By the age of seven years, most children are fairly proficient (though not yet mature) in fundamental motor skills, and start to use these basic motor skills until they improve both qualitatively and quantitatively. They also learn to vary, modify, and combine them into transitional motor activities. For example, they combine running with jumping, running with kicking the ball in different ways, or running (like a sprinter or a soccer, football, or field hockey player) with the ball under control.

This last phase is precisely where the Soccer Development Model begins. This ensures that the children are exposed only to the level of activity for which they are ready. Children from the specific or sport movements phase should be exposed to the first level of the Soccer Development Model, then follow the suggested plan step by step and in the timeline indicated.

The Five Levels of Progression

The Soccer Development Model comprises five different formation levels:

Level 1   Games for basic abilities and capacities
Level 2   Games for mini-soccer
Level 3   Games for 7-on-7 soccer
Level 4   Games for 8-on-8 soccer
Level 5   Games for official 11-on-11 soccer

These levels represent a progressive sequence of exercises and simplified games supplying the most common game situations for this age group. There may be fewer players, reduced dimensions in the playing field, fewer or less-complicated rules, and so forth. Young soccer players progress slowly from one unit or game to the next one and are continually confronted with slightly more complex and difficult problems. They progress to the next level only after understanding and mastering the technical and tactical requirements of the previous simplified game or competition. *Their training thus becomes a developmental process of gradually increasing demands.*

The step-by-step approach, both for players and their coaches, is one of the keys of success in this method. Each segment is broken down into a series of small steps, leading gradually and methodically to the final goal of each level of accomplishment or formation: being able to perform well in the respective competition of that particular age group.

Moving step by step, you may travel great distances.

At the first level, youngsters aged seven years and up encounter a games program of basic abilities and capacities. These include multilateral games; juggling and balancing the ball; dribbling; passing, receiving, and shooting; and tackling. They are exposed to simplified competitions (like the soccer decathlon and triathlon) and a great variety of multilateral games. Through them, children have sufficient opportunities to practice and discover varied motor skills prior to and during their acquisition of soccer-specific skills.

After completing the different multilateral tasks, the children progress to the second level. This level comprises a progressive series of simplified games for teams of two players, in which the children not only experiment with and improve in the correct use of the skills learned in Level 1, but also build up their capacities in communication and cooperation. The objective of this level is to understand and learn to successfully play the Level 2 competitive "mini-soccer" (first 3 on 3 without a goalkeeper, then 3 on 3 with a goalkeeper) and the "3-on-3 Triathlon."

All proposed activities in Level 3 (simplified games 3 on 3, 4-on-4 Soccer Triathlon, and the development of young goalkeepers) lead to the capacity of playing 7-on-7 soccer across the width of the official field.

At Level 4 the players mainly encounter a program of simplified games for teams formed by four and five players. Here they will consolidate skills, with help from the activities of the first three levels. They chiefly employ corrective exercises and develop their reading and reacting skills, which allow them to perform well in 8-on-8 soccer between the penalty areas of the official field.

At Level 5, presented in a second volume (available only in Spanish: *Fútbol a la medida del adolescente [Soccer for Adolescents]* published by Federación Andaluza de Fútbol, Sevilla, 1999), the adolescents ready themselves to play the full game.

In the first level of the Soccer Development Model, children practice fundamental skills like dribbling, passing, and shooting.

Level 1
(generally for boys and girls 7 years and up)

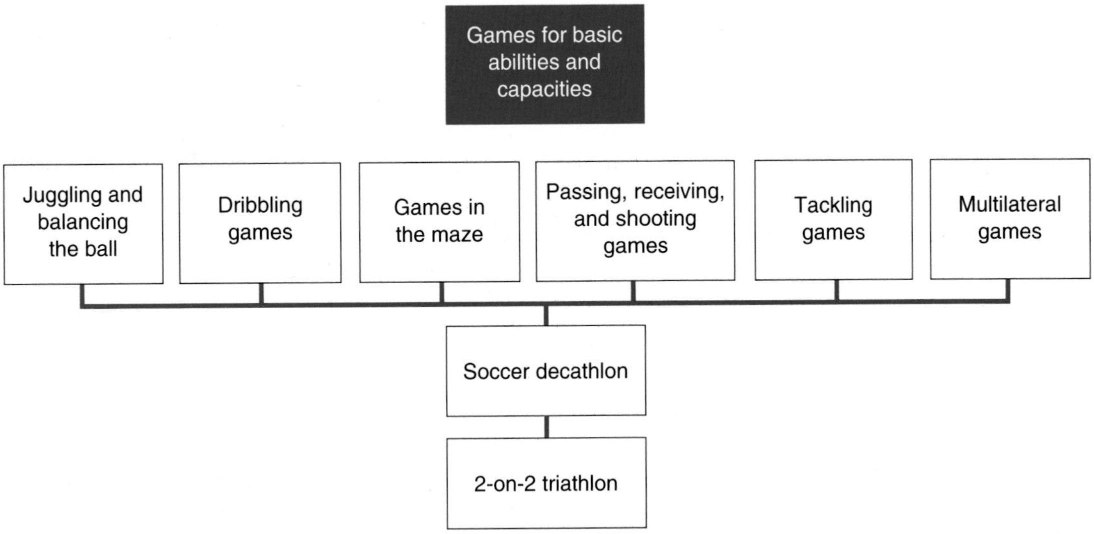

Games for basic abilities and capacities

Juggling and balancing the ball	Dribbling games	Games in the maze	Passing, receiving, and shooting games	Tackling games	Multilateral games

Soccer decathlon

2-on-2 triathlon

Level 2
(generally for boys and girls 8 years and up)

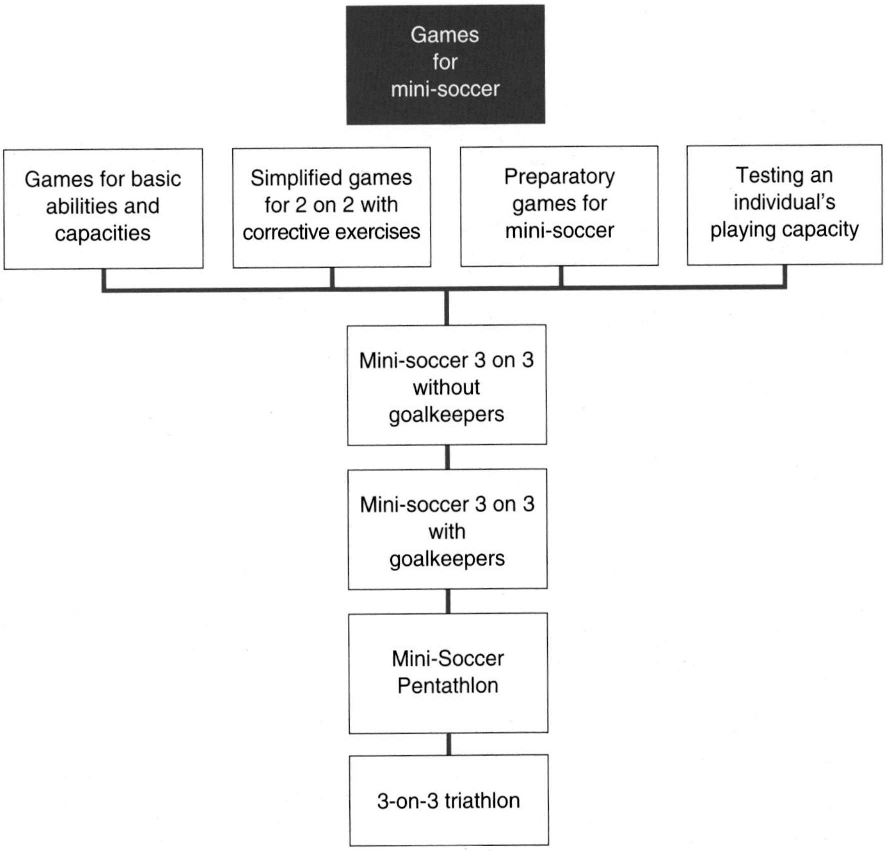

Games for mini-soccer

Games for basic abilities and capacities	Simplified games for 2 on 2 with corrective exercises	Preparatory games for mini-soccer	Testing an individual's playing capacity

Mini-soccer 3 on 3 without goalkeepers

Mini-soccer 3 on 3 with goalkeepers

Mini-Soccer Pentathlon

3-on-3 triathlon

The Soccer Development Model contains individual exercises and simplified games as well as collective and complex game situations.

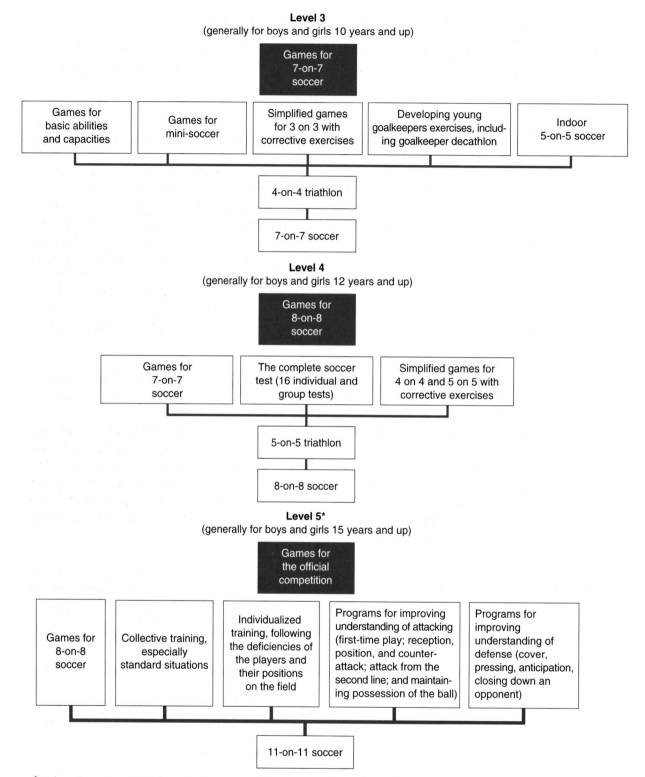

Level 3
(generally for boys and girls 10 years and up)

Games for
7-on-7
soccer

| Games for basic abilities and capacities | Games for mini-soccer | Simplified games for 3 on 3 with corrective exercises | Developing young goalkeepers exercises, including goalkeeper decathlon | Indoor 5-on-5 soccer |

4-on-4 triathlon

7-on-7 soccer

Level 4
(generally for boys and girls 12 years and up)

Games for
8-on-8
soccer

| Games for 7-on-7 soccer | The complete soccer test (16 individual and group tests) | Simplified games for 4 on 4 and 5 on 5 with corrective exercises |

5-on-5 triathlon

8-on-8 soccer

Level 5*
(generally for boys and girls 15 years and up)

Games for
the official
competition

| Games for 8-on-8 soccer | Collective training, especially standard situations | Individualized training, following the deficiencies of the players and their positions on the field | Programs for improving understanding of attacking (first-time play; reception, position, and counter-attack; attack from the second line; and maintaining possession of the ball) | Programs for improving understanding of defense (cover, pressing, anticipation, closing down an opponent) |

11-on-11 soccer

*Information on Level 5 is presented in a second volume, currently available only in Spanish: "Fútbol a la medida del adolescente," published by Federación Andaluza de Fútbol, Sevilla, 1999.

Advantages of the Development Model

There are many advantages to implementing the Soccer Development Model. It will benefit not only your soccer coaching but also, more importantly, the young players themselves.

Link Between Training and Competition

Each level is composed of various corrective exercises and preparatory games especially designed to match the different tasks that competition demands of the players in each age group. Solid bridges are constructed between learning a subject and correctly applying it moments later in a simplified training game or the official competition. Training and competition are always seen as a unit, one being tightly linked to the other. This differs from traditional methods that often deprive children of an efficient training and learning process. An efficient process fosters understanding of the game which is fundamental for a good performance. Instead of focusing mainly on *how* to execute a closed skill, the Soccer Development Model coaches children on how the skill should be best *applied:* when, where, and why. This assures that the players are always highly motivated because they see the training practice always in function of the game and not isolated from the competition (as observed all too often among youth soccer players).

Increase in Successful Actions

Players who take part in competitions specially designed for their age (mini-soccer 3 on 3 and 4 on 4; 7-on-7 and 8-on-8 soccer) will have far more successful actions than in the traditional game, thereby leading to an increase in self-esteem.

The game of mini-soccer played with only three players per team is manageable for 8-year-old beginners and, with an additional goalkeeper, for 9-year-old ones. In the same way, the players under 12 years consider the seven-member team game as the right challenge and the under-14 players understand the game with eight players per team (which develops between the two penalty areas of the official field). The following table provides a brief description of this progression. Each game is explained in much more detail in following chapters.

Logical Progression of Youth Competitions

Age at start of season	Number of players	Substitutes allowed	Ball	Duration (periods × min.)	Rules of the game	Dimensions of the pitch	Age of the referee
8	3	1	No. 3	3 × 10	No offside 4 goals Rolling substitution	25 × 35 m.	Under 16
9	4	1	No. 4	3 × 10	No offside 4 goals Rolling substitution	25 × 35 m.	Under 16
10–11	7	3	No. 4	2 × 25	Goals 6 × 2 m. Rolling substitution	35 × 55 m.	Under 18
12–13	8	3	No. 4	2 × 30	Goals 6 × 2 m. Rolling substitution	Between penalty areas	Under 20
14 and up	11	5	Official ball (No. 5)	2 × 45	Official rules	Full field	No age restriction

Enjoyment of the Game

Naturally, when players execute more successful actions, they enjoy the game more. Every two years the difficulty and complexity of the competition is increased in perfect harmony with the growing physical and intellectual capacities of the players. When young players progress with the help of the Soccer Development Model from so simple a base and in such small increments, the occurrence of significant failure is out of question. Enjoyment and confidence in their capabilities become the driving force for the players' motivation and further progress. *A correct use of the model reinforces success, whereas the traditional way of subjecting children to the difficulty and complexity of the full game only reinforces failure.* As success reinforces success, failure reinforces failure.

Unfortunately, most people still associate great performance with pain, struggle, and exhaustion. In soccer, the idea that learning can be fun is still novel. Whatever is enjoyable seems to be forbidden. Even though playing is the mode in which children discover their world, too often the moment they get on the training ground, the joy of discovery is quashed.

The following illustration represents the difference between the current way of coaching and the coaching method suggested by the Soccer Development Model. Presently, most children struggle to meet the demands of a competition geared toward adults. However, with the game tailored to a child's development and gradual progress to more complex activities, the youngsters can experience much more success and, most importantly, they enjoy the game.

In the future, soccer competitions should be tailored to match a child's gradual physical and intellectual development.

Ease of Application

Players aren't the only ones who reap the benefits of the Development Model. The model provides coaches with a complete and effective training plan that can easily be applied to their players. Applying the Development Model gives even the most inexperienced soccer coach the ability to gradually, yet effectively, guide young players into the full game of soccer. The result is already known: more intelligent and complete soccer players.

To become more familiar with the Soccer Development Model, teachers can even attend a weekend-long refresher coaching course. (For more information, send an e-mail message to **horstwein@redestb.es**.) In such a course, coaches learn the reasons behind a particular training and competition program for a particular age group and how to implement that program. Coaches not only acquire a detailed knowledge of the model's contents and what objectives to achieve with each exercise or simplified game, they also become familiar with the most effective methods and coaching style to apply.

Fixed Goals

To make the model as useful as possible to the coach, it has been structured in a hierarchical order, both with overall objectives (for example "Games for Mini-Soccer") and specific, partial aims (for example "Dribbling Games" or "3-on-3 Triathlon") for each level. For each game or exercise, specific goals have been identified. Having the goals fixed for each category provides these benefits:

➤ Gives coaches guidelines for structuring and developing the training and learning process and allows them, after assessing the content, to add their own training programs to those proposed in the model

➤ Helps link the proposed program to the fixed goals

➤ Adds incentives for the children, allowing them to focus their efforts on some definite objective, without having to guess why they are playing some way or what they are aiming toward

➤ Allows coaches to discover whether they are achieving the objectives and to make any necessary alterations

With the objectives clearly defined and fixed for each category of children's soccer—one of the key elements of this unique teaching and learning model—the children are not exposed to a training process in which mere improvisation and intuition on the coaches' part determine content. The development model incorporates relevant sport science and motor development research in its program. This way, countless correct habits are developed in the early years of learning, resulting in the desired improvement of performance at higher levels.

Most youth coaches teach several days a week, without knowing whether they are doing it right or not. For them, their old habits, acquired long ago, are comfortable; they've used their old methods frequently without much thinking. When exposed to the simple and effective training programs of the Soccer Development Model, however, they might well double their effectiveness, doing a better job in less time and with half the effort.

Coaching Philosophy

Without the right coaching philosophy, the Development Model will take you only so far. Coaches should always maintain a healthy, positive attitude during training and competition.

Philosophy During Competition

These are some basic principles that all coaches should apply during competition.

➤ For boys and girls between 8 and 14 years old, always consider playing well as more important than winning. While learning to play, the participants must forget about the result of the game. They should be encouraged to take some risks, despite the fact that this kind of play might allow the opponents to score. Players, parents, and coaches should consider competition only as another kind of training.

➤ Mobilize all your efforts to reach victory, but never look to win at any price. Victory should never be considered the only important thing to achieve.

➤ Don't mind losing a match, because defeat is always a possibility when competing; there is no guarantee for winning. If another team beats yours, it's generally because of their better play. It should never be because your team didn't put all its efforts into the game to win it. As long as you have tried hard and played up to your capability to prevent the defeat, you never should feel like losers.

➤ Winning isn't as important, nor losing as bad, as most parents believe. It all depends on what a team was able to demonstrate. Players may win after having showed a poor game played in a destructive manner—and they may lose despite having played much better than the opponents and having enjoyed every minute of the game.

➤ Learn to play in a competition as though it is a matter of practice and to train with the spirit of playing an important competition.

➤ Winning is only a consequence of playing well. That is why every player has only to look to give his or her very best. The result will fall like a ripe fruit falls from the tree.

➤ In all youth categories up to 14 years, coaching to win a match is easier than coaching to play the game well. Playing well allows you to discover new solutions to old problems, again and again. Teaching to win, on the other hand, means you limit and restrict the game mainly to those already known skills and tactical moves that are important for winning it (like long clearances, "kick and rush" philosophy, pressing defense, etc.). Yet when you compete this way, in the long run you also restrict and limit the complete formation of the young players.

"If you want to win, you almost have to forget about winning."

L. Morehouse/L. Gross

Coaching Characteristics

Certain characteristics can help a coach become well-accepted by their young players (also see Halliwell 1994). Here are some of those identifiable characteristics:

- Previous experience and successes as a player
- Previous experience and successes as a coach
- Pleasant appearance, in physicality as well as in dress
- Correct (healthful) lifestyle (habits)
- Correct proceedings in work: punctuality and efficiency
- Good organization of training sessions, meetings, travel
- Good communication level: knows how to explain concepts and also how to listen

A good coach has the ability to observe and analyze players' movements and correct mistakes.

- Good disposition—always has time for the players
- Ample knowledge of techniques and tactics and how to coach them
- High motivation for passing his knowledge on to the players through questioning
- Positive approach—encourages and motivates players with positive remarks, creates enthusiasm, praises frequently
- Knows to coach from the bench: readjusts his team's play through quick decision making, changes players shrewdly, has a sense of humor
- Can exercise leadership in the dressing room as well as on the ground during training and matches
- Self-control—emotionally stable, transmits calmness and serenity, especially when conflicts arise
- Desires to improve constantly—looks out for new exercises and games as well as for new coaching methods or styles, self-critical in his coaching
- Capacity to observe, analyze, and correct mistakes or wrong habits
- Honest and fair with the young players—doesn't favor any particular player, demands a lot but is fair to everybody
- Open to any suggestion—stays flexible, listens to the suggestions of his players and assistants
- Demonstrates true interest in his players (and for their problems off the playing field)

Maintaining a Positive Attitude

A coach of young soccer players should conscientiously do and say things that make the young players feel good, accepted, important, happy, and successful.

Try these simple gestures:

➤ A warm greeting, using the player's name
➤ A smile
➤ A thumbs-up sign
➤ A pat on the back
➤ Talking with players
➤ Playing some games or activities with them
➤ Asking their advice and listening to what they say
➤ Helping them learn something new or to improve something
➤ Helping players adjust their personal objectives
➤ Attending to all their questions
➤ Showing interest in their friends, family, and hobbies
➤ Providing fun and enjoyable activities
➤ Giving encouragement
➤ Praising, avoiding criticism
➤ Including the youngsters in the teaching process through effective questioning

Combining the right coaching philosophy with the step-by-step progression in the Soccer Development Model is a surefire formula for success. The experience of success in the tailor-made competitions is a great motivator for progressing even further, but so long as the federations, clubs, and schools are not aware of the necessity to introduce this logical progression of competitions, improvement will not take place. When more federations decide, at no expense, to provide for each youth category a proper annual competition, more children will have the opportunity to play well and to enjoy the game.

PART II
Coaching Players 7 Years and Up

The first two levels of the Soccer Development Model aim to introduce young boys and girls to the game of soccer and foster their interest in the sport. Before coaches can apply the games and exercises at these levels, however, they must be aware of the specific characteristics and needs of their young players.

Soccer Players Under Age 10

Children who are younger than 10 years of age have some significant characteristics:

➤ They still lack fine motor skills.
➤ Their movements are usually whole body actions, with little accuracy.
➤ They have short bursts of energy and enthusiasm.
➤ Developing coordination, they still are clumsy.
➤ They play or participate for fun, for enjoyment.
➤ Their actions are not yet automatic or programmed.
➤ They are unsure what actions lead to success at a skill.
➤ They see every detail as being important.
➤ They are uncertain in their actions and in how to achieve desired outcomes.
➤ They lack a clear idea or model of the new skill.
➤ They cannot follow too many instructions or handle too much information at one time.
➤ They are unable to use feedback information effectively.

By being aware of these traits, coaches can tailor their teaching to meet young players' characteristics and needs. The following table lists additional characteristics of young children and coaching strategies that should meet the youngsters where they are in their development.

Tailoring Coaching Practices to Match Young Players' Characteristics

Characteristic	Coaching Strategy
Boys and girls under 10 share similar characteristics when it comes to sports.	Boys and girls should train and compete together.
The children are highly motivated and enthusiastic. They like to be active.	Maintain their motivation through a wide range of exercises and games. Avoid queues and players being stationary. Listen to what players say.
Children under 10 are generally egocentric and like to possess the ball the maximum time possible. They are very concerned with themselves.	Provide everybody with a ball. Plan competitions 1 against 1 in order to make maximum use of this egocentric phase. Promote fair play.
Players have not yet established a "motor pattern" that allows the skills to be executed without thinking. Their whole attention is directed toward the ball.	Allow time to learn skills. Improve the skills through repetitions and vary them before you evaluate the skill level through a competition, which demands a correct execution. Design drill practice to avoid excessive decision making.
Everybody enjoys scoring. Scoring gives self-esteem and confidence.	Practice simplified games as well as mini-soccer with its variations so that everybody scores and plays the ball frequently.
Attention capacity is limited. They are unable to process a lot of information.	Change activities frequently. Mix specific soccer exercises or games with multilateral games. Almost every 15 minutes vary the content and let them compete with only one substitute. Don't talk too much; it's better to demonstrate without talking at the same time. Introduce one thing only.
They are just starting to learn how to cooperate.	Select games in which cooperation leads to winning (like mini-soccer). The demands on the players should not exceed their stage of development. Ask questions to involve the young players mentally.
They have no clear idea of an ideal performance and therefore rely entirely on their coach.	Demonstrate to allow the young players a source of feedback.
They are sensitive to criticism and failure.	Under all circumstances be positive. Praise and reward often to reinforce an effort or an improvement.
They are less tolerant to heat and cold than are adults.	Ensure that they wear adequate clothing. They lose fluid quickly.

Game Alterations for Beginners

In the same way that coaching strategies should be modified when working with young beginning players, so too should certain rules of the game, including the weight and circumference of the ball, the dimensions of the playing field, and the size of the goals.

Size of the Soccer Ball

Instead of using balls of regular size and weight for all children, regardless of their age, it's better to adapt the circumference and weight of the ball to the height and strength of the young soccer players. Children under the age of 8 should play with a No. 3 mini ball, which weighs less than 340 grams (12 ounces). For players between 8 and 13 years of age, using the No. 4 ball, which weighs between 340 and 370 grams (between 12 and

13 ounces) and has a circumference of 63 to 66 centimeters (25 to 26 inches), encourages better and quicker learning during practice sessions and competitions. For comparison, the official ball weighs between 400 and 454 grams (between 14 ounces and 1 pound) and has a circumference of 68 to 71 centimeters (27 to 28 inches). Experience has shown that even 13-year-old players feel more comfortable and capable with a No. 4 ball than with the regulation ball of official size and weight, which may ideally be reserved for youths 15 years and older.

There are many advantages to using a smaller ball. Because they weigh less, the smaller balls can be passed over longer distances, allowing children to play more like adults. This undoubtedly stimulates their perceptive capacities to a higher degree. Using the No. 4 ball places higher demands on visual skills, including peripheral vision, dynamic visual acuity, and vision in the depth of the field.

The No. 4 ball also makes it possible for players even farther than 15 meters away from the ball carrier to actively take part in the game. In addition, the frequently observed clustering of players around the ball, characteristic of play at these age groups, is observed less often, compared with youngsters using the official ball approved by FIFA. If players don't cluster around the ball, their observing, analyzing, and decision making is made easier; they can reach a higher level of play with fewer ball losses.

During the first four years of practice with young players, a coach should often insist on their using the less-skilled foot. Thanks to the introduction of the No. 4 ball size, all the activities presented in Level 1 of the Soccer Development Model (as well as many exercises and games of Level 2) can be carried out with the "wrong" foot, opening a much wider range of playing options that makes the game more attractive to the players.

Because the official ball is oversized and too heavy for young players, many children struggle not only to handle the ball in training and competition, but may even incur a knee condition called Osgood-Schlatter's disease. This syndrome is characterized by pain, swelling, and tenderness just below the knee, over the shin bone. However, with the smaller, lighter ball, players can move more naturally and in correctly executed movement patterns. The result is that they can acquire new skills much easier and avoid injuries.

Dimensions of the Playing Area

The drills and games contained in the first level do not require an entire soccer field. An area approximately 20 by 40 meters is needed, that is, less than a quarter of the area of the full field or even a basketball court.

When you organize a simplified game for two teams, as coach you should always take into consideration that *the less skilled and capable your players are, the wider and deeper the dimensions of the playing area* should be. A small area often doesn't allow the player sufficient time to observe and analyze the game situation and then make a quick decision on which skill to execute, why to execute it, and when and where to do it best. The smaller the area, in fact, the more demands are put on skills and on attention. Needless to say, a larger playing field facilitates successful play.

If only a small playing area is available, you must reduce the number of players taking part in the game. You compensate with this reduction for the lack of space, in other words, still trying to tailor the game perfectly to the young players' abilities and capacities. If all the players cannot be directly involved in the practice because of limited space, the "extras" may carry out some additional activities while they wait. For example, they might practice juggling or balancing the ball outside the training area, shooting it against a fence or wall, or even executing exercises for improving their level of coordination and balance with and without the ball.

In brief, it is important for coaches to select the correct dimension of the playing area—based on the technical, physical, and intellectual performance levels of their players and on the number of players involved in the game.

Size of the Goals

The size of the goals also plays an important part in the teaching and learning processes with young players. To create a game of control, the rules of many simplified games require beginners to control the ball in the opposing wide goal area (between 6 and 20 meters wide). Wild shooting is not desirable! Players should handle the ball gently and with care, without using violent movements.

Wider goals help stimulate a young player's perception. For beginners (who generally direct most of their attention toward the ball) a wider, uncovered space between the cones is much easier to detect during the dribble. In addition, using wide goal areas gives the wings the same opportunities to score as a center forward has, thus leading to the habit of always attacking with sufficient width. Last, with the use of wide goals, players do not tend to cluster around the goal. Thanks to having wide goal areas for practice sessions, young players have greater enjoyment in the game and their self-confidence increases.

Structuring a Training Session

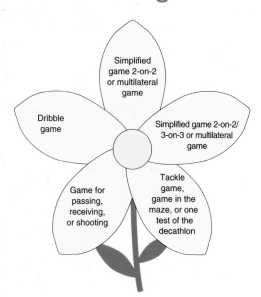

Structuring a training session for beginners is comparable to tearing off a flower's petals one by one, always starting and finishing with the petal labeled "simplified or multilateral game."

It is not only the quality but also the variety of the activities that determines the degree of success and acceptance of the practice session and its contents. Just as someone in a restaurant orders a tasteful and varied meal after having studied the menu carefully, the coach should create an effective and enjoyable coaching session for beginners by selecting various activities from the menu. For example, at Level 1 a coach chooses from a variety of games focused on basic abilities, creating a "menu" of several courses:

Aperitif—one of the simplified games for two-player teams or, if the beginners still are not ready for that, a multilateral game

First course—a dribble game with one or two variations

Second course—a game for passing, receiving, or shooting

Dessert—a tackling game, a game in the maze, or a test selected from the decathlon

After-dinner drink—a multilateral activity or simplified game for teams of not more than three players

To ensure a high level of attention from the beginners, it's best to change the proposed activity every 15 minutes. A coach should also alternate exercises and games of great intensity with those making less physical demand.

The games and exercises in the Soccer Development Model are not to be done in any rigid order. It is up to the individual coach to put together a combination of exercises that is right for his or her players.

Now that you know how to adapt the game to fit the abilities, interests, and expectations of players under 10 years of age, it's time to expose them to the games and exercises in Level 1.

3

Games for Basic Abilities and Capacities
Level 1

"Hidden in every human being exists
a child that wants to play."
Friedrich Nietzsche

The first level of the Soccer Development Model has the important task of introducing children from 7 years and up to soccer and developing their interest in and love for the game. If coaches, during these decisive years of children's development, fail to give their young pupils adequate training tools and stimuli to enable them to play with confidence and enjoyment, they may convert their young charges, now full of potential, into future second-class athletes. Coaches should always aim to support the healthy and harmonious development of the children who start out motivated to practice their favorite sport. The less rigid and more varied their teaching style and the training program they adopt, the more pleasant and comfortable the atmosphere will feel to children.

In this chapter, you will be introduced to a variety of games that form Level 1 of the Soccer Development Model. These games are not to be done in any rigid order; instead, you can assemble a variety of games and create a training session that works best for your group of players. With adequate exposure (at least twice a week) to these games, beginners quickly gain their first experiences in such basic game situations as these:

➤ Dribbling the ball
➤ Receiving, controlling, passing, and shooting the ball
➤ Taking the ball away from the opponent
➤ Considering their teammate(s) or opponent(s) in attack as well as in defense

Not only will children be exposed to special programs that focus on the correct execution of the fundamentals in simplified game situations, but the youngsters will also take part in the Level 1 competitions—the decathlon and the 2-on-2 soccer triathlon—that have been specially adapted to their developmental phase.

Level 1 of the Soccer Development Model introduces young children to soccer and strives to develop their interest in and love for the game.

Because they are so egocentric, few seven- and eight-year-old beginners are capable of successfully playing team games. Every player likes to be the protagonist of the game and tries to keep the ball in his or her possession for as much time as possible. The games and exercises in the first level have been designed with this in mind.

Juggling and Balancing the Ball

In addition to developing their overall coordination and motor skills, young beginners should be introduced as early as possible to an array of exercises and games. The activities should help players learn to juggle and maneuver the ball in all possible situations on and off the field using any part of their bodies.

Two training sessions a week in the club or school are insufficient for players as young as seven years to develop a ball sense that will give them an extra edge. They should spend several hours a week during their leisure time juggling with different sizes of balls until they learn to handle and control the ball in all possible situations. With a little fantasy and creativity, all kids and their coaches can invent appropriate programs using partners, walls, nets, and other resources.

Dribbling Games

Dribbling games help players develop the ability to carry the ball on the ground with balance, footwork, speed, change of direction, and coordination. These techniques are key to further discovery of the beauty of soccer; possessing them allows players to quickly reach a satisfying level of play.

Although you will find the next section of games (as well as later programs) numbered to represent a progression from easier to more difficult exercises and games, that doesn't mean that you must follow the activities in order. Presenting a more complex problem on occasion challenges the more talented players, while using easier exercises gives the less talented youngsters the confidence and motivation to try harder.

I. Parallel Lines

The coach establishes two parallel lines set 2 meters apart. Two players stand side by side on the first line, facing the second line. When the coach signals, both players dribble their ball down to the second line, then turn around and dribble it back. The first player to dribble the ball 10 times across both parallel lines wins. To maintain control of the ball while changing direction, the player should experiment with the use of different surfaces (exterior, interior, the sole, and the heel) of both feet. Which technique assures the quickest turn?

VARIATIONS

➤ The teacher varies the distance between the parallel lines, up to 5 meters.

➤ None of the players should touch their ball in the central zone formed by the two parallel lines. Start with a zone that is only 1 meter wide and later extend it to 2 meters, 3 meters, then 4 meters.

➤ The ball must be played with the less-skilled foot only.

2. The Tunnel

Two players face each other at a distance of 1 meter. Player 1 has 30 seconds to pass the ball as many times as possible through the tunnel formed by the separated legs of Player 2. The first player kicks the ball through the partner's legs and then runs behind Player 2 to return-kick the ball to the original side. Meanwhile, Player 2 remains still and counts the number of goals scored by the opponent. Then the players switch roles, and Player 2 gets 30 seconds to pass the ball. The winner is the player who, using either the left or the right foot, passes the ball more often through the tunnel formed by the opponent. In case of a tie, repeat the test.

VARIATIONS

➤ The player who forms the tunnel stands in a neutral zone of 2 meters. The player with the ball passes it from outside of the zone through the opponent's legs, using either the left or right foot. The stationary player counts the number of goals scored in 30 seconds from outside of the neutral zone. Both players then alternate roles until both have competed twice. The winner is the player who scores the most goals in the two attempts. In the event of a draw, repeat the activity.

➤ Immediately after a goal is scored, the player who forms the tunnel changes the position of one "goalpost" (one foot) by pivoting and changing directions.

3. Eyes Up While Dribbling

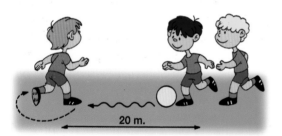

20 m.

This exercise is done with three players. Player 1, the ball carrier, dribbles to Player 2 who is about 20 meters away. While dribbling the ball, Player 1 lifts his head as often as possible to be able to count the number of fingers shown by his teammate (Player 2) in front of him. The latter, after having received the ball, practices the same dribbling and lifting his head to count, but goes in the opposite direction, while Player 3 indicates different numbers of fingers. The coach should make sure players practice dribbling the ball with either foot.

VARIATION

➤ Various players dribble their ball in both directions around a square (5 meters per side), going continuously into and then immediately out of it, using either foot. The goal is to avoid a clash with other players who dribble in and out of the square in the opposite direction.

4. Avoiding Collisions

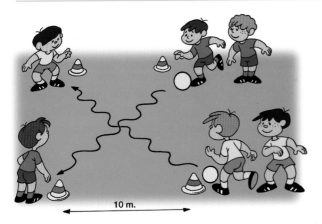

To start, two players must dribble their ball to the opposite corner (about 10 meters away), trying to avoid each other player while crossing the path. The players waiting at the opposite corner return the ball using the same diagonal path. First the practice is carried out with two balls and four players, and later the intensity and difficulty are increased by using four balls and involving eight players at the same time. To avoid injuries, do not organize any competition between the teams!

5. Precise Passing

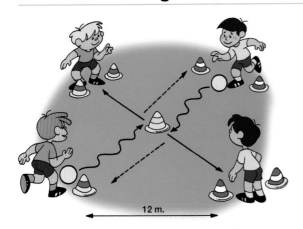

Four players pair up and form a square, the partners (Players 1A and 1B; Players 2A and 2B) adjacent to one another. The two players in diametrically opposite corners (Players 1A and 2A) each have a ball. At the same time, they start to dribble the ball on the left "driveway," or imaginary lane that is left of the cones, until they reach the cone in the center. From there they pass the ball on the run with the right foot, passing it leftward to carry the ball through the cone goal on the left. That goal area is occupied by their partners (Players 1B and 2B), who now proceed the same way in the activity. The first pair to score 10 goals wins.

VARIATIONS

➤ Before executing the pass, the player has to carry out a dummy pass in the opposite direction.

➤ To introduce triangle play (wall passes), the receiver has to return the ball immediately into the run of the passer who runs into the opposite goal. After 10 triangle passes both players change functions. Later on, both players practice with an initial pass to the opposite side.

6. Black and White

Players line up and are separated into two teams facing opposite directions. Each player has a ball. Practice first without the ball, then with it. Upon the coach's signal, all players dribble a ball until they cross the far lines. A team wins if all its members cross their end line with their balls under control before all the other team's members cross their end line.

VARIATIONS

➤ The teacher designates one team as dribblers. While the dribblers try to reach the proper end line dribbling their balls, the other team (now without balls) chases the attackers, trying to prevent them from dribbling their balls across the end line.

➤ Both teams face each other, from a distance of only 4 meters apart.

7. Zigzag

Set up the field as shown in the illustration. Have the children first practice their running and turning techniques without using a ball. Players run from the starting line to the second line, then return to the starting line and run to the third line, returning to the second line before running all the way to the finish line. Next have the players dribble the ball as they run the same zigzag course. You can organize a competition, splitting players into two performance levels to motivate them all. All the lines must be passed with the ball under control.

VARIATION

➤ Use a relay with three-player teams. Set up cones and balls as illustrated. Player 1 on each team collects the first ball placed at the first cone (1) and carries it to the third cone (2). After its deposit, she returns without the ball to catch the second ball from the second cone (3) and dribbles it two cones farther (4) to place it beside the fourth cone. Continue in this fashion to the final line. After having deposited the first ball at the fifth cone, Player 1 runs to touch her teammate at the opposite side who does the same zigzag path through the cones, running in the opposite direction. The first team to finish the course correctly wins.

8. Changing the Square

Set up teams of four youngsters each, giving each a ball. Form squares (see the illustration), the corners marked by cones. The children should practice first without a ball and later with a ball. Every time the coach gives a visual signal, each team's players run (without and later with the ball) toward the next square, keeping control of their balls. As coach, give them an instruction or a visual signal to run either in a clockwise or counterclockwise direction. (Be sure to make it clear which way to run as most very young children don't know the terms clockwise and counterclockwise). The team that manages to control all their balls first in the next square wins. Running with the ball in opposite directions should be avoided because of danger of head injuries through collisions!

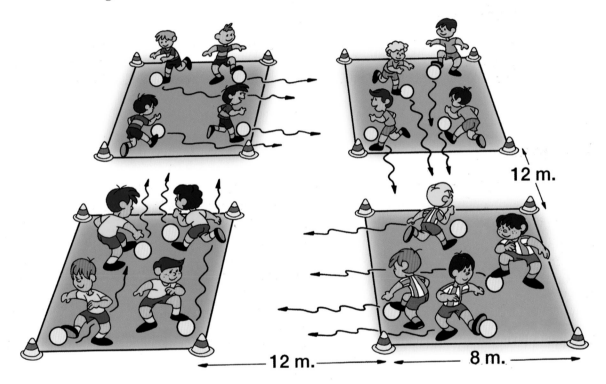

VARIATION

➤ Have a defender situated between the squares. This child tries to delay the opponent's attack and conquer at least one ball. He or she then must dribble that ball into the square from which the attack was launched.

9. Twice Around the Square

Youngsters do this activity in pairs to practice running and dribbling skills around a square (see illustration). Have players first practice the course without the ball and then with the ball. Two players located at opposite corners of the square simultaneously start to dribble, going twice around the square in the same direction (clockwise or counterclockwise). Practice and competition should be carried out in both directions to ensure that all players learn when to use the left or when to use the right foot. The coach should explain good technique and then question them.

➤ When should the ball be "carried" close to the feet?

➤ How might an attacker save time?

➤ Which foot should be used in the change of direction when running clockwise (counterclockwise)?

VARIATIONS

➤ After having completed half of the way around the square, the attacker must turn around at the second cone and return to the starting point.

➤ Set up a course for "Around the Triangle": mark off an equilateral triangle and set up four cones along one (the base) side of it (see illustration). Children compete in pairs. Both competitors start from different locations around the triangle. As they get to the base of the triangle, they must dribble in and out of the four cones before dribbling up the next side. They learn to dribble with either foot and to execute different techniques of the dribble using different surfaces.

10. Bandit

Mark the field in squares with cones to establish four "home bases" with four balls in each. The bases should be at least 10 meters apart from one another. Form four teams per playing field, each team made up of just two players. After you give a visual signal to start, players steal balls from other teams' home bases and deposit them at their own base. No tackling or defending of the home base is allowed. The team with the highest number of balls after 30 seconds of play wins the game.

11. Occupying an Empty Goal

This activity is something like a soccer version of "Musical Chairs," a game that most children already know. Mark off a circle, about 15 meters in diameter, using about 10 cones to create the inner and out edges of the path. These cones also designate five goals. Give each player a soccer ball. Six players at a time dribble their ball in any direction around the circle formed by the five goals. After you give a visual signal, all the players try to occupy one of the five empty goals. Whoever doesn't succeed loses a point.

VARIATION

➤ Use the same setup as above, but designate a neutral defender who makes the task of the attackers even more difficult.

12. Pivoting

One player, a "receiver," stands 3 meters behind a 3-meter-wide cone goal, facing a teammate who feeds him a 10-meter pass. The receiver runs toward the traveling ball with the intention of receiving and controlling it in front of the goal. Once he gains control, he dribbles the ball sideward to one cone and then, with a sudden change of speed, turns toward the other cone, making sure he is always placing himself between the ball and the imaginary defender (represented by the cone goal). Once he has rounded the goal, after one or two direction changes, he turns and penetrates through it.

13. Staying in the Shade

When there is plenty of sun and long shadows, pair up children and have one be an attacker, the other a defender. Designate a line between them. Position the defender so that the sun is directly behind the youngster, producing a good shadow. The attacker tries to maintain the ball for as much time as possible in the shadow of the defender, who continuously moves toward the left and right side in front of him but stays beyond a line drawn between them—which the defender is not allowed to cross. It helps to first practice this shadowing without the ball to improve their body positioning, balance, and footwork. In order to train the defender's footwork, he finally tries to shadow the attacker's ball with the aim of not allowing even a ray of sun to "burn" the skin of the ball.

14. Practicing the Drag

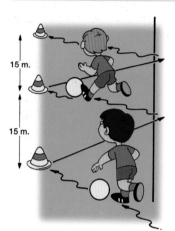

Give each of the players a ball and set up cones in a row for each child to designate a running course (see illustration). Each player carries the ball toward a cone (representing an imaginary defender), then drags it square to the right side and collects it after a change of speed and direction at a distance of about 3 meters. Explain to the youngsters the idea of dummy moves and feints, and have them practice executing the dummy moves. First practice from left to right, later from right to left.

15. Drags From Left to Right

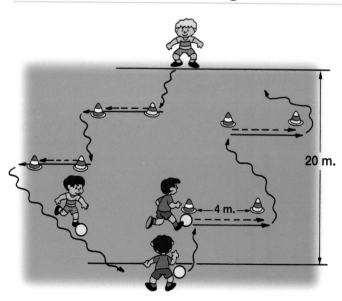

Position eight cones as shown in the illustration to mark off the drag areas. Explain to the children that they should experiment using different techniques to beat an opponent, including different kinds of body or foot dummies during the execution of the drags. To stimulate the young players' fantasy and creativity, the coach declares the player with the finest technique (no technical mistake) or the most original dummy as winner.

VARIATIONS

➤ Practice drags from right to left (see illustration). The attacker should always dribble the ball first toward the right cone before dragging it suddenly, with one touch only, toward the left one. Once the ball runs beyond the level of the left cone, it should be collected after a quick change of speed.

➤ Drag the first goal from left to right, and the second from right to left.

➤ Drag the first cone goal from right to left, and the second one in any direction you wish.

➤ Drag against "handicapped" defenders who remain inside the goal area (between the two cones) with one foot always keeping contact with or touching the goal line (see illustration). First the defender should be outplayed with a drag from left to right, then from right to left, and then with the decision left up to the individual player.

➤ The defender in the second goal indicates through his position (putting weight clearly on one foot) on which side the attacker should beat him. This activity helps youngsters learn to always observe the defender before attempting to beat him with a drag. The attacker must also learn to stay out of the defender's range of action.

16. Playing 1 on 1 in a 5-Meter Square

Mark off 5-meter squares with cones. Pair up the youngsters, designating an attacker and defender for each pair. To start, the attacker and defender stand at diagonally opposite corners of the square. The attacker scores when he manages to control the ball across one of the two red goal lines in front of him. Before using the ball, have the children first practice the game without it—as a game of tag—to work out optimal body position, balance, and good footwork.

VARIATION

➤ Give a visual signal for both players to run once around the square, starting from their diagonally opposite corners. The player who first completes the full turn then runs into the center of the square to pick up the stationary ball and dribble it, as in the previous game, before carrying it across one of the two goal lines.

17. Avoiding the Tackle From Behind

Pair the youngsters, designating an attacker and defender. The playing field should have two lines, set about 15 meters apart. In this game the attacker with the ball has the objective to dribble it across the opposite line without losing possession of it to a defender. To start the play, the defender is 1 meter behind the attacker, aiming to tackle from behind or from a side. But once the attacker dribbles the ball for at least 5 meters, she may choose to go backward and carry the ball across the starting line. In reaching either line, she gets a point.

To get free of the defender behind her, the attacker may

➤ turn around, shielding the ball with her body,

➤ sell him a ball-stop dummy, using a backward change of speed to control the ball on the end line in front of her, or

➤ cross with the ball into the run of the defender before the latter can reach her. In the moment of crossing diagonally in front of the defender, he is forced to slow his speed.

18. Chasing the Dribbler

Outline a square on the playing field with four cones. Direct two players to diagonally opposite corners outside of the square. Only one of them has a ball; the other player chases the ball carrier around the square. During the first trial (Level 1) the defender has the task to touch the attacker with one hand. Later (Level 2) he is to touch the ball with either foot. For every cone reached with the ball under control, the attacker gets 1 point. The attacker learns to improve his play by dribbling the ball out of the reach of the defender whenever the latter gets near him.

VARIATION

➤ Play this game of Chase the Dribbler with four players: two attackers and two defenders. Give a visual signal for each defender to start from the cone directly behind his attacker, aiming to immediately pressure him. The defender should try to prevent the attacker's concluding a run around the square (award 1 point for a successful defense). Defenders and attackers switch functions until one of them scores 5 points.

19. Hot Pursuit

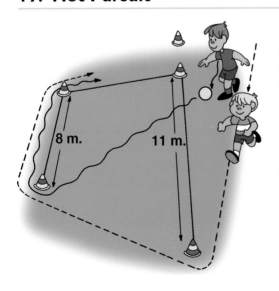

Mark off a trapezoid on the field, with four cones set at slightly uneven distances as in the illustration. A fifth cone serves to form the goal line with the first cone. Children play in pairs, one being the attacker and one the defender. The attacker dribbles the ball around a triangle formed by three cones. As soon as she begins, the defender reacts and follows her, trying to prevent the attacker from keeping the ball under control as she reaches the goal at the end of the circuit. The defender, however, has a handicap: he must run a longer distance (around all four cones) in order to catch the attacker. Every player attacks and defends five times. The winner is the player who, after having completed the dribble around the cones, controls the ball more often in reaching the goal line (cones 1 and 5). In case the result is a draw, hold a playoff.

20. Avoiding a Tackle

Designate a rectangle for the playing field, two of the sides twice as long as the other two. Each child has a ball. While all five players are controlling their own balls, they also all try to dispossess any other player with a correct tackle. Any good tackle that disposes an opponent (or plays the ball out of the square) counts as 1 point. In case one player loses the ball, that child returns into the square and continues the game until someone has reached 5 points.

VARIATION

➤ Tackles count only if they are executed with the left foot.

21. Cops and Robber

Mark off a square as shown in the illustration. Group the children into threes, with one called the "robber" and the other two "cops." Children play to see how many seconds the "robber" can control his ball within the playing space against both policemen, who also must control their balls while trying to catch the robber's ball. The stress conditions of this game give players the chance to practice lifting the head while dribbling the ball, applying dummies, quick changes of direction, and speed, as well as their capacity to stay out of the reach of a defender. It's good training to practice first without the balls.

VARIATIONS

➤ Perform "Cops and Robbers" as a relay in two fields side by side. Team 1 positions its robber in the first field ("A"), while its two policemen chase the robber of Team 2 in the second field ("B"). Team 2 meanwhile positions its two cops in Field A. The two policemen who first catch their assigned robber are called winners.

➤ Use the same 20-meter square and pairs of youngsters, each with a ball. Without leaving the square, each attacker tries to maintain possession of the ball for as many seconds as possible against an active defender. After five trials to establish a record, the attacker and defender switch functions. First try out this game without a ball, as a game of tag; then practice with the ball to learn to systematically apply dummy moves and to protect the ball with the body against a defender. After each turn, the two competitors should have a complete rest.

22. Maintaining Ball Possession

Mark off the playing field as in the illustration, at first making it about 15 meters square and later a rectangle of 10 by 15 meters. Divide the youngsters into groups of four players: within a group, three children are attackers, each with a ball, and the fourth is the defender. None of the players may leave the playing area. The defender tries to dispossess the attackers of the ball. The attackers, in turn, try to "escape" or prevent the dispossession. The defender tries to get near enough to the attackers to push as many balls as possible out of the square within the playing time, which is 30 seconds.

While dribbling, the attackers learn to lift their heads to see the defender, change speed and direction to keep away from him, and shield the ball in order to avoid his tackling successfully.

23. Cat and Mouse

Mark off a small square (2 meters), and pair up the youngsters into "cats" and "mice." The pair first practices the game without balls. Then give each pair a ball. The "mouse," persecuted by the "cat" (the attacker), tries to remain in possession of the ball for 20 seconds without stepping inside the square. After three rounds of the attacker gaining possession of the ball, the players switch so that the cat becomes the pursued mouse. To make the game more difficult, as players improve, lengthen the playing time to 30 seconds and make the off-limit square only one meter on each side.

This game helps young players recognize how perception and the capacity to execute dummies at the right instant are as essential as dribble techniques to winning. It also helps them develop speed and coordination.

24. Escape

This game involves up to seven pairs. Each of the players should be given a ball which he or she has to dribble within a center circle on the playing field for 7 on 7 (50 to 65 meters long by 30 to 45 meters wide). Each player has to challenge the opponent assigned to her, once you call on a team to start or give a visual signal (for instance, wave a colored card). Each member of that team must then dribble his or her ball out of the circle, trying to control it until getting across one of the 7-on-7 field's sidelines or, later, score from inside either penalty area.

The players of the team not called leave their balls behind and instead chase their personal opponents, trying to dispossess the ball carriers and return with the balls to the center circle.

25. The Challenge

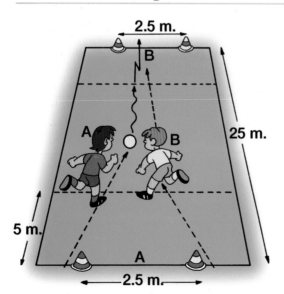

Set up the rectangular field with four cones to mark off the two goal areas; use one ball for every two youngsters. Pair up the children. Two players stand on the same goal line (A), one on the right post (cone) and the other at the left of a 2.5-meter-wide goal. After you have given a visual signal, both should run toward the ball placed in the center point of the playing area at a distance of 12.5 meters.

The first player to gain its possession must dribble it into the opponent's shooting zone (B) and score. While Player A at the left post (cone) tries to score at the far goal, Player B at the right post, once he or she gains the ball, must dribble it through the open goal from which he or she started. If these and other soccer rules are broken in the midfield, the defender resumes the game without the ball, from half a meter behind the attacker. If the defender infringes the rules in his own shooting zone, he will be penalized with a free kick from the center of the playing area through the opponent's empty goal. Each time a goal is scored or the ball runs across any end line, the two players change their starting places. The winner is the first player to score two goals.

Games in the Maze

There are two program activities referred to as Games in the Maze: the "Dribbling Maze Game" and the "Passing Maze Game." The first activity serves to stimulate the young players' perception capacity, their sense of orientation, their capacity to make quick decisions, and their coordination and dribbling techniques with both feet. Because of these many skills to be developed, it is useful to have more variations to ensure plenty of practice and to sustain interest. The second activity in the maze, along with its variations, helps improve the skills of communication and cooperation between the passer and the receiver.

1. Dribbling Maze Game

Set up the playing field according to the illustration, establishing eight 1-meter goal areas using two cones for each. Pair up the children and give each a ball. Two players start simultaneously but across from each other at positions outside the maze. Their task is to dribble the ball in any direction through all eight goals of the maze without skipping any. The winner is the player who returns to the starting point first—with the ball under complete control. Have the youngsters practice without the balls at first. Later, more than two players may compete at the same time.

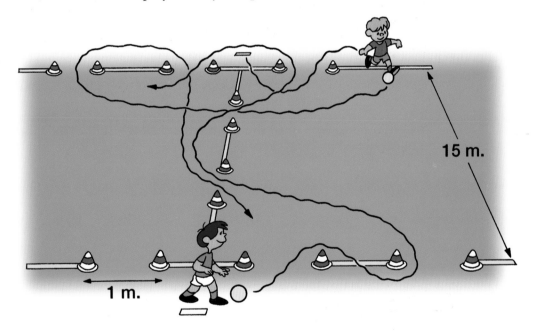

15 m.

1 m.

VARIATIONS

➤ Instead of goals, players will form tunnels. After the ball is played through a tunnel, the attacker has to jump over the tunnel.

➤ Try the game as an activity to see which player needs less time to run through six different goals. Have the players use only the less-skillful foot or to complete a full turn before dribbling the ball across a goal line. You might also ask players to dribble the ball backward through the cone goals.

➤ To score, the players must pass the ball through a goal (tunnel) and collect the ball behind the goal without running through it.

➤ To win the player must pass through as many different goals as possible within 10 seconds.

➤ Set up eight goals with cones of at least three different colors. During the dribble the players have to look out for the position of the goals with the color you call out or designate. The winner is the first player who runs the ball through eight goals without repeating the same one immediately after having scored in it.

➤ Two or three players dribble their proper ball through any of the eight goals, while two or three other players enter the maze without a ball to modify the position of some cones. This forces the attackers to continuously look up and adapt to the new situation.

➤ Before the ball is dribbled across a cone goal, the attackers must complete a half turn with the ball (turn until the player's shoulders point toward the goal). After that the player turns halfway back (toward the left or the right) into the original position and then dribbles the ball across the goal line. The youngster must be sure that during the pivoting motion his or her body is always placed between the goal line (two cones) and the ball, thus learning to shield it later from an opponent.

➤ Three players occupy three of the eight goals, thus demonstrating to the four attackers that they can score only in one of the five unoccupied ones. The defenders may move from one to another goal but may not tackle at all. The winner will be the attacker who first scores at six of the goals without repeating the same one twice in a row.

➤ Four attackers play against two defenders who may tackle (unlike the previous variation, which prohibited tackling).

➤ To score, the attackers must slightly lift their ball with either foot above an obstacle (or an outstretched player) on each goal line.

2. Passing Maze Game

Set up the playing field for a maze, as shown in the illustration, which has different spaces between goals. Divide the youngsters into pairs (a passer and a receiver) who will use passing to score goals. The pair that manages to score in six different goals first will win. Make sure that the player moves behind another goal immediately after the pass to make himself available for the next pass. Explain that the players must establish a visual agreement between passer and receiver before the pass is executed. Apply the same variations as with the "Dribbling Maze Game."

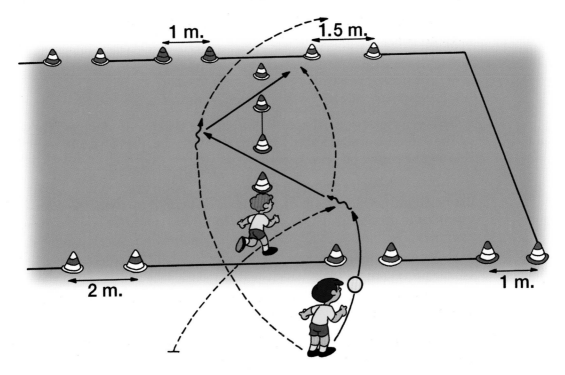

Passing, Receiving, and Shooting Games

In addition to accurate passing, good control of the ball from teammate to teammate is of paramount importance: it provides a team the opportunity to maintain or instigate their attacking moves.

The high percentage of failure in passing and receiving is a consequence not only of technique but also of other errors occurring immediately before the ball is passed or controlled. These are some typical errors:

➤ There is no visual agreement between the passer and receiver.

➤ The receiver doesn't make himself available at the right instant when the passer is "ready" (poor "timing").

➤ The receiver waits for the ball instead of running to it.

➤ The players show poor passing skills (the ball was passed too softly, too high, or imprecisely, or the pass was executed too late).

For a player to control the ball in the particular game situation, even a youngster, he or she should learn and apply commonsense principles to a variety of techniques. Teach your young players the following:

1. Watch the ball carefully until it touches your feet or body. Also pay attention to the position and movement of your teammates and opponents before and after the execution of the control. The more experienced and confident you are, the more you can assimilate and process other relevant information while focusing on the ball.

2. Try to position your body in line with the ball as soon as possible. If you're an attacker, for example, it is relatively easy to receive the ball as you face the proper goal, but often this isn't effective for creating a goal opportunity: it's too slow, and it limits your ability to play the ball quickly into the opponent's penalty area. Therefore you should learn to receive and control balls from a side position as well, which allows you to perceive your teammates' and the defenders' position and movements in the space between you and the goal.

3. Make a cushion for the ball with your feet or any other part of your body. Don't be tense. Relax and incline your "playing" knee or the body slightly forward. This helps your control. Receive the ball in a balanced position at the point of collection. Being balanced well makes for having successful control with subsequent movements. And it allows a receiver to deceive any opponent nearby with a body feint.

4. Position the ball during the control for the next play. If you are the receiver, you should already know what to do next before the ball is controlled. You must select what technique you'll use for the control of the next move: a dribble, a shot, or a pass. It's paramount to be able to execute an intentional or purposeful control for continuing with the attack. Learning this principle of ball control will help any player to perform considerably better.

The culmination of a good pass is perfect control of the ball.

The games in this section are designed to enhance the players' ability to maintain control and make accurate and well-timed passes with different techniques. They learn to calculate and anticipate the direction and speed of the ball while receiving and controlling it, including how to read the direction and speed of an opponent's pass. The children first practice passing a stationary and then a moving ball without indicating its direction. They also learn to receive the ball to exploit and utilize it for their next action.

I. Against the Wall

Station the youngsters near a wall, at a distance of 4 to 7 meters. They pass the ball to the wall from this point. How many flat passes can be executed against the wall without lifting the ball? To make this activity a competition, the winner is the player who manages to execute five passes against the wall without having to move more than 1 meter away from his original position.

Use also the left foot or alternate one pass with the left foot and the next one with the right foot. Insist that youngsters use different surfaces of the foot when passing. Have them repeat the activity, trying to establish a personal record time.

2. Going for Distance

Position the children along an end line, each with a ball. Each player shoots his ball from the end line into the depth of the full soccer field, then follows after it and continues kicking it deep until reaching the opposite end of the field, finishing the run with a shot on an open goal. Which player's ball travels farthest? Who needs the fewest shots for scoring a goal? Have the youngsters also use their less-skillful foot and experiment in shooting with different techniques. Ask them to describe their experiences.

3. Accurate Passing and Control

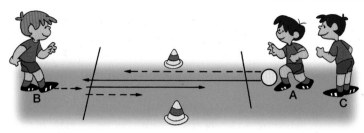

This game can be played by individuals or as a team competition with three players per team. Each player has to score from a distance of 6 to 9 meters through a 2-meter-wide goal area (marked off by cones) and then have a receiver (B) be able to return the pass to the third player (C). The passer (A) follows the pass to the other side and awaits a pass from the third player (C). Whoever first scores 10 goals with the passing technique you instruct them to use is the winner. With a team, the winning three players can be either those who first score 10 goals or those who score the most goals within 30 seconds.

Explore what constitutes the most efficient passing technique by using effective questioning with the players.

VARIATION

➤ The third player (Player C) becomes a goalkeeper and defends a 4-meter-wide goal area (marked by two cones) in the center between the two teammates. The attacker who doesn't manage to score has to switch position with the goalkeeper. As coach you may ask the attackers to shoot stationary or moving balls. Also ask them to use the drop-kick technique or the volley shot from different distances to also experiment with these techniques.

4. King of the Penalty

Divide the youngsters into groups of three for this game. You should have a 7-on-7 goal area (6 by 2 meters) for each group playing. The three players involved start with 5 points each. The oldest among them is the first to defend the goal area, while the other two players stand 9 meters away to attempt kicking in goals. For every effective goal, the defender loses 1 point. When an attacker fails to score, however, she changes her position and function with the goalkeeper. A player wins when the opponents have lost all their points (caused by the winner's more accurate and powerful shots).

VARIATION

➤ Indicate what technique the players must use for each set.

5. Torpedoes

This game takes 10 players and five soccer balls. Choose four players to line up next to each other along a line, each of them in possession of a ball. The same number of players stands facing them at a distance of 9 meters (you can move this distance back to 11 meters as the youngsters gain experience); the children in this other line do not have a ball. Two other players position themselves outside the "tunnel" at either end, like an entrance and exit. One of the end players has a ball, and these two pass each other that ball. The players forming the tunnel who are in possession of a ball try to calculate and anticipate the direction and speed of the ball going through the tunnel from end to end. They each try to "torpedo" it by kicking their ball at it accurately and with the correct speed. If they miss, the player across the way will receive the pass. The kickers can use either foot. The receivers try the torpedo as it returns to the original end player.

6. Quick Goals

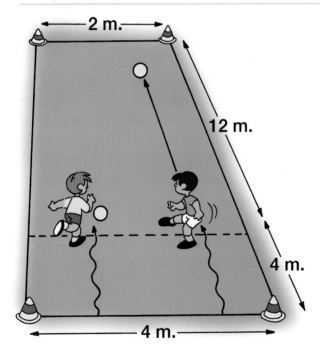

Pair up the children and give each a soccer ball. Set up a long rectangle (see illustration), using four cones to mark the corners; the end of the rectangle serves as a goal area and should be only 2 meters wide. Give a visual signal for the two players to set off. They must dribble their ball at least to a 4-meter line and then shoot it from there into the goal area, another 12 meters away. The player who first manages to pass his ball from any point beyond the 4-meter line between the far goal posts scores a point. The winner is the player who scores the highest number of points in five attempts.

When shooting under time pressure, the players ordinarily may choose their technique. As variations, however, you can insist they use a particular technique or play the ball with the less-skillful foot.

7. Passing and Receiving 1 on 1

Pair up the players and mark off playing fields (see illustration) for them with cones. Every two players share a ball. The ends of each field should form goal areas (8 meters across). The players each stand in their own goal area, which they must defend. Player 1 tries to pass the ball along the ground from his goal line toward the opposite goal. To avoid Player 1's scoring a goal, Player 2, the defender, learns to read the direction and speed of the opponent's pass. Then they reverse the action to pass the ball back to the original line.

Shots above shoulder height are disallowed and don't score. For any infringement (using hands or leaving the goal line) a penalty is awarded from the center of the playing area. Instill faking the direction of the pass. The first player to score four goals wins the event.

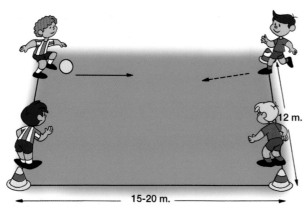

VARIATIONS

➤ As practice, count only passes played along the ground as scoring.

➤ Have the children try this competition using the less-skillful foot to pass.

➤ Have the receiver start from a point 2 meters behind his goal line. This helps develop the good habit of running toward the ball before controlling it.

➤ Have the children practice passing and receiving 2 on 2 (see illustration). Pass the ball across the opponent's goal line from the spot where it was controlled. Depending on how much explosive power the four players have, you can mark off the goal areas to measure up to 12 meters wide and the distance between them can be increased to 15 to 20 meters in length.

8. Disguising the Pass

Set up pairs of cones to mark off two goal areas (each 2 meters wide; see the illustration). These goals should be about 11 to 13 meters from the starting line. A receiver stands behind the goals and a third player (designated as the defender) stays just in front of the goals, very close to them and facing the player who is passer. Players have five passes to try to score a maximum number of goals in one of the two goals areas (first with a stationary ball set on the ground). A pass through one of the goals is considered valid only when the second attacker behind the defender can manage to control the well-placed pass.

As the children improve in passing, decrease the distance between the goals (which is, at first, 4 meters). More experienced players can also practice passing with a moving ball (without indicating its direction).

9. Soccer-Tennis

Position the children near a wall and give each pair a soccer ball. Play "soccer-tennis" against the wall, the youngsters passing the ball alone or in pairs to hit above a line indicated on the wall. Have the children systematically use their less-skilled foot.

VARIATIONS

➤ Players assume a side position in relation to the wall, standing about 6 to 8 meters away from it. They dribble the ball parallel to the wall and pass it in the air against the wall to pick up the rebounded ball on the run a few meters later. This way the children simulate a "triangulation," initiated with a pass on the inside or outside part of the foot. They should practice standing in a direction so that the wall is to their left and then right side.

➤ Ask the players to invent other exercises for improving their ball sense and acrobatic skills!

10. Passing Around a Square

This game involves groups of five children playing around a square marked by four cones. Besides developing accurate passing skills, the players learn to receive the ball in a way that helps their next play (the next pass) and to speed up the ball's movement by their using appropriate positioning in relation to the nearest cone, the execution of "purposeful controls," and hard passes.

For this game, the children stand as in the illustration, to take turns in passing the ball around the square. Competition in either direction and with flat or high passes is permitted; you may allow each player any number of—or only two—ball contacts. The passer must always follow the run of the ball. Use a stopwatch to time individual players or set up a timed competition between several teams at a time.

VARIATION

➤ Add a sixth player to create a competition between the five passers and a sixth player who, in the moment of the first pass, must run twice around the square. The competition is between the runner and the ball to see who completes the two laps sooner! The sixth player is not allowed to play the ball. The six players take turns being the runner to vie against the other five passers. All the children should take a turn at being the runner.

11. Shooting Circuit

Of six children, four dribble and shoot and two act as goalkeepers at the end goal areas. Mark off an area as in the illustration with two opposite goal areas that are 4 meters in width. The players dribble the length (20 meters) to enter the goal area in front of them. Once he or she crosses that line, the player must immediately shoot at the defended goal. After the shot on goal, the attacker becomes goalkeeper; this former goalkeeper takes the ball and lines up in the next goal area at the right (or left) side. He or she then does the same as the first attacker, dribbling in the opposite direction, again on the right (or left) flank. The winner is the player who scores the highest number of goals within 5 minutes.

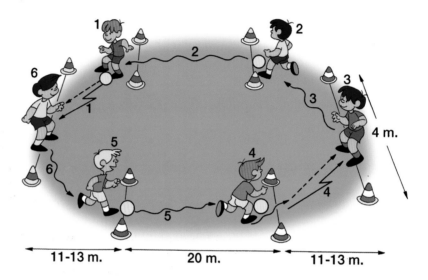

12. Shooting Circuit Variation

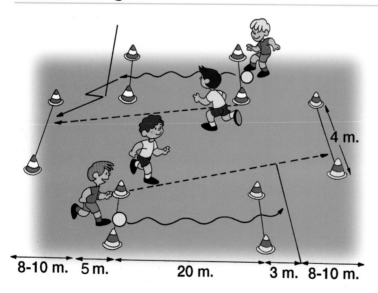

See the previous activity. Several pairs compete simultaneously in opposite directions, first clockwise and later counterclockwise. One player is in possession of the ball and the other one is the goalkeeper situated just 4 meters in front of him. When the attacker touches the ball, the goalkeeper tries to position himself as quickly as possible at the goal in front of him before the attacker is able to shoot from a point within that shooting area of 3 meters. After the first attack, both players change functions and practice on the other side of the circuit. Whoever scores more goals within 5 minutes wins.

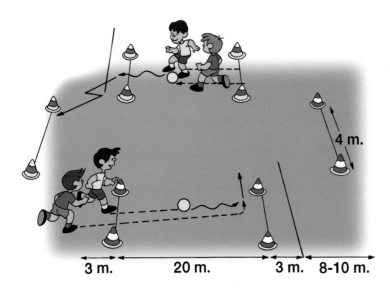

VARIATION

➤ Here the defender places himself 3 meters (after some experience with this game, you can decrease the distance to 1 meter) behind the attacker to his right side. Once the attacker touches the ball within the first pair of cones, the defender may follow him with the objective to clear or take the ball before it can be shot from a point inside the shooting zone toward the next undefended goal.

13. Precise Passing to Both Sides

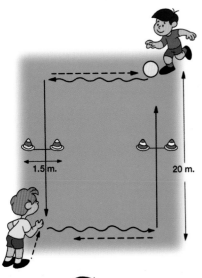

Set up the playing field with two pairs of cones marking off goal areas about midway on either side (see illustration). Pair up the players and give each pair a ball. Indicate what technique you want the players to use for passing. Player 1 starts out with a 15- to 20-meter dribble, taking her level with the goal cones. There, she centers the ball through the cones still at a distance of 10 meters. Player 2, meanwhile, waits there to receive the ball behind the goal. Then the receiver (Player 2) dribbles and centers through the other goal. After every pass the player returns to his or her starting point (see the dotted arrow) and receives the other player's pass. Whoever first scores 10 goals wins.

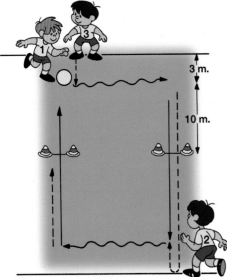

VARIATION

➤ Play the same game with three players. After each pass of the ball through the center, the passer follows the direction of the ball (see illustration's dotted and solid lines) and awaits a pass from where his receiver awaited his pass. The players take turns as indicated by the numbers in the illustration. Also reverse direction to practice centering from the left to the right. Instill passing with the less-skilled foot and with the ball on the run. The distances for passing must be adapted to the children's level.

14. Putting the "Wrong" Foot Forward

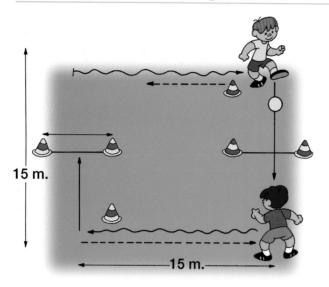

A pair of players uses one soccer ball for this game. After dribbling the ball the length of the field, the player must pass it while on the run through the goal area marked by cones set 1 to 1.5 meters apart. If the ball has stopped, the pass is not valid. After executing the pass from the first cone to the goal area, the player returns to his starting point and waits behind the other cones to receive the second player's pass. The winner is the player who first scores five valid goals from a distance of 5 meters.

You can change the distances, depending on the performance level of the players and whether they are using the less- or the more-skilled foot.

15. Passing Across a Wide Zone

Group the youngsters in teams of three players. Set up the field to indicate lines about 20 meters apart, and explain that the area between is a neutral zone. Two players, one with a ball, stand on one line facing a third teammate standing on the other line. Player 1 passes the ball across the neutral zone to Player 3 who should immediately return it to Player 2. None of the players may step into the neutral zone to pass. After a pass, each player must follow the ball. Among the different teams, the winning one is whichever can make 10 passes across its neutral zone.

16. Playing 3 on 3 Across the Opposing End Line

Form two teams of three players each. The teams face each other in the separated playing areas (as in volleyball). Without leaving the team's part of the playing area and without dribbling the ball, one of the three players tries to pass the ball along the ground across the opposing end line, despite the defense efforts of the three opponents in the other team's part of the playing area.

No high passes are allowed. When the ball runs out of the playing area, it should be reintroduced at the spot where it went out. Touching the ball more than twice or with the hands is penalized with a goal.

17. Scoring Against One Defender

Have the children pair up and practice on either side of an open 7-on-7 soccer goal. Place cones to form a 3-meter-wide goal at the top of the penalty area (at 11 meters). The defender passes the ball with speed from the end line toward the cones forming that goal. Once the attacker has managed to control the ball in front of the goal cones, he should score against a neutral goalkeeper and the defender who followed his initial pass.

Question the youngsters frequently to help them understand (1) the best way to receive the ball (ideally, the ball should rebound into a position that allows a quick shot toward the goal), (2) how to best play out the defender (on his weak side, with a well-tempered pass past him, with a tunnel between his spread legs, or when he is stationary and in a frontal position), and (3) the most efficient way to defend in this situation (to close down the attacker and force him to score with his less-skillful foot).

After every three attacks, the two players change positions and functions. You might later have the attacker start from 2 meters behind the cone goal to encourage his or her running toward the oncoming ball.

18. Scoring With 2 on 1

Again use a setup with a 7-on-7 soccer goal but have the children form groups of three. At the instant a pass is made by the attacker from the penalty area line to his teammate situated on the end line, the defender near the receiver tries to distract the receiver. The attacker tries to receive, control, and play the ball on his own or with a return pass. The 2-on-1 situation finishes with the ball going out of the penalty area, an offside infringement, or a goal being scored despite the presence of a constant, active goal-keeper. All the players practice five times in each of the three positions. For every goal scored, both attackers gain a point.

VARIATION

➤ For more advanced players, the attacker passes the ball from the goal line to his teammate at the top of the penalty area. Once the quick pass is made, the receiver runs toward the ball to control it—despite the active play of the defender who is initially behind him. At the same time both players (attacker and defender) on the goal line move into the penalty area where they establish a 2-on-2 situation. The attacker's aim is to score a goal, and the defenders try to clear the ball out of the area.

19. Scoring With 3 on 2

Again use a field with a 7-on-7 soccer goal. Designate three youngsters as attackers and position them about 20 meters away from the goal. They should assume the positions of inside forward and center forward. Designate two youngsters as defenders and one as a goalkeeper. The attackers have 10 seconds to score. More advanced players learn not to run into an offside position.

VARIATION

➤ One attacker, situated with the ball on an imaginary 20-meter line, passes to one of the two teammates who are close to the end line. Both the teammates are marked by two defenders. Once the ball is passed, the three forwards try to resolve the 3-on-2 situation to their advantage and score a goal. Of course, at the same time the two defenders, with help from the goalkeeper, do everything to gain possession of the ball and pass it back to you, the coach, as you follow the development of the game from a position close to the third attacker.

20. Shooting 1 on 1

The game is played on a basketball or mini-soccer field (use dimensions of 20 to 25 meters by 35 to 40 meters) with 7-on-7 soccer goals added. Form two teams of two players, using just one soccer ball. One player on the team is the goalkeeper, and the other attacks or defends, depending on the game situation. Every 2 minutes the goalkeepers change their positions and functions with the field players.

VARIATIONS

➤ Each team's sole attacker gets support from two teammates, who stand beside each goalpost of the opponent's goal. They are only allowed to play the ball with one touch, and they may not enter the field. After every three goals scored by any team, all four players change positions and functions.

➤ Play 3 on 3 with goalkeepers, but without restrictions.

21. Playing 1 on 1 With Shot on Goal

Again use a mini-soccer field (20 to 25 meters by 35 to 40 meters) with two goals on each end, and form two-player teams. Each player may play in only one half of the field. The aim is to score from inside the shooting zone in one of the two opposite goals. Start the game with a ball toss. Every 2 minutes the players of each team switch positions and functions.

22. Game of Accurate Passes

Set up two small squares (see illustration) for the playing field. Eight players participate in two groups of four, using one soccer ball. Three players are stationed in one of the squares; they maintain possession of the ball against one defender until one of them is able to pass the ball across a neutral zone (about 10 to 15 meters) to a second square. There three other players are offering themselves for a pass, which that square's defender tries to intercept. Once an attacker managed to receive and control the ball, his or her team works to return the ball to one of the three attackers in the opposite square. Count up the number of successful passes in a 2-minute game. The less experienced the young players are, the larger the playing area should be.

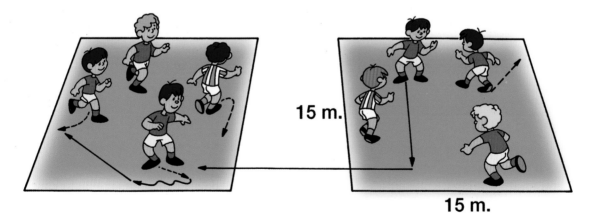

23. Head Kick Into the Goal

2 m.

Youngsters do this activity in pairs, using a No. 3 soccer ball. The play area should have a 7-on-7 goal set up. The two players face each other at a distance of 2 meters. One of them, the goalkeeper, throws the ball in an arc toward the forehead of the other, the attacker. The attacker does everything to score with a "head kick" against the goalkeeper, who must remain on the goal line. If the ball is not conveniently served, the attacker may refuse to play it with his forehead. After five headers, the players switch positions and functions. The winner is the player who scores more goals.

Tackling Games

A smart player attempts to tackle an attacker in possession of the ball only when she is almost certain of success. If there is any doubt, she delays the tackle or executes a dummy while retreating and waiting for a more convenient instant to recover the ball.

A player should only attempt to tackle the ball when there is a great chance of success.

The defender should not only exercise patience and assiduously study what tackling methods lend the highest percentage of success in particular game situations but also develop these tactics:

1. Avoid running toward and into an attacker who controls the ball
2. Use dummies to generate situations that give you an advantage
3. Carefully observe the speed and trajectory of the ball
4. Select the best line of approach, placing yourself closer to the goal than the attacker
5. Vary the method or type of tackle
6. Avoid being flatfooted before and during the tackling
7. Make sure, in case of necessity, that a second or a third tackle could be executed
8. Keep the legs bent before executing the tackle
9. Reduce the speed of the attacker who has complete control over the ball
10. Be mentally prepared to attack in case your tackling succeeds
11. Surprise the opponent (a slow tackle lacks surprise)
12. Deprive the attacker of time and space, forcing the player to make mistakes
13. Remain in a balanced position when defending, without crossing one leg over the other

The tackling games in this section teach players how to position themselves correctly in relation to the attacker, to tackle with precise timing and with patience. Furthermore, they'll learn to execute dummies and switch quickly to attack after making a successful tackle. By doing these activities in the progressive order you find here, players develop their defensive fundamentals step by step, before engaging in more complex situations.

1. Touch the Rope

In this first game, the children do not use a ball so that they can concentrate on learning a correct succession of movements. Pair up the children into defenders and attackers. The defender faces an "attacker" who holds a rope in his or her hand; the end of the rope touches the ground 1 meter in front of this child. The defender's objective is to use just one explosive step forward in order to touch or stamp on the rope before the attacker can move it away. The defender has five chances to achieve his aim using either foot. Then the players swap roles. The defender quickly learns to assume an optimal basic position before tackling. In this position the legs should be sufficiently bent to keep the point of gravity sufficiently low. Apart from learning this correct succession of movements, the children experience how important quickness and surprise are for success in tackling.

2. Tackling a Loose Ball

Again group the players into pairs (defender and attacker) and mark off two lines on the field. Each defender tries to touch with a quick tackle (using either foot) the stationary ball lying close to the feet of the attacker 1 meter in front of him. The attacker, without looking at the ball but instead at the defender's feet, should move the ball aside in the instant the defender steps in. Players rest for at least 5 seconds between attempts. After five attempts at touching the ball, the players switch roles.

3. Tackling Twice

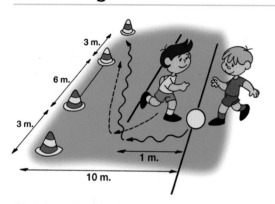

Set up two 3-meter-wide goals with 6 meters between the goals and two lines as in the illustration, and have the children play in pairs. The defender stands 5 meters away from the goals, about in the midway point between them. The attacker faces the defender, standing 1 or 2 meters in front of the defender with a stationary ball. At the instant the defender tries to tackle it with speed and surprise, the attacker plays the ball sideways, out of the range of action of the defender, and then tries to dribble it through one of the two goal areas.

As soon as the defender has failed with his frontal tackle, he must quickly recover his basic position and try to tackle (this time in a side position) for a second time—and prevent the attacker from controlling the ball in one of the two cone goals. Each player must defend his goals during five attacks.

The winner is the defender who allows the attacker to score fewer goals. After each tackle, the children should rest at least 10 seconds.

4. Tackling Against a "Limited" Attacker

Group the children in pairs, giving each pair one soccer ball. A defender faces an attacker who dribbles the ball straight to him. When the attacker is about 3 meters in front of the defender, the latter steps slightly to the left until his right shoulder "faces" the right shoulder of the ball carrier who dribbles the ball straight to his right side without being allowed to dodge him.

Once the ball is level with him, the defender, now in an optimal side position, executes a quick and technically correct tackle. Defenders should take care to first touch the ball, and not the foot of the attacker.

In this activity, the defender gains experience in optical-motor assessment. The child learns to tackle at the very best instant, not too early and not too late.

VARIATIONS

➤ The defender must carry out a step-in feint once the attacker is about 3 meters in front of him or her. Immediately after this obvious dummy, the defender recovers, again assumes an optimal basic position (but no longer in front of the attacker), tackles quickly, and tries to surprise the opponent from a side position.

➤ The defender steps completely to one side, allowing the opponent to penetrate. After this quick turnaround, the defender adapts to the attacker's speed and stays with the opponent, shoulder-to-shoulder, until the ideal instant arises for tackling. This usually is when the ball is away from the attacker's feet. Any tackling from behind should be avoided (to not infringe on the game's rules). Tackling in retreat against a "limited" attacker should be taught while having the attacker on defender's left (and also on the right) side. It's best to practice this activity first without a ball and then with it to help improve the basic position, the channeling of the opponent, and the retreat side-on-side with the attacker.

5. Intercepting Passes

Gather the players in groups of fours. Two players face each other at a distance of 15 meters, passing the ball between them on a line. Two defenders, at either side of the running line of the ball and always about 2 meters away from it, try to intercept the pass. The interception should be practiced from different positions [with the left (or right) shoulder of the defenders pointing to the ball carrier, or with the defenders facing the passers].

6. Five Tackles

8 m.

The children again work in groups of four players. Three players each dribble a ball within a small square (8 meters by 8 meters), while a fourth child without a ball has five chances to tackle. The defender's aim is to clear as many balls as possible out of the square within these five tackles.

Besides observing the attackers carefully during their dribbling, the defender must have the patience to tackle only when a good opportunity arises. Executing dummy tackles will allow the defender to achieve a higher percentage of success. The player with the highest rate of successful tackles (out of the five possible) wins.

VARIATION

➤ All four players are in possession of a ball, and they all try to tackle the ball of any of their three opponents while controlling their own ball. When a player loses the ball, he or she must quickly collect it to continue participating in the game. Whoever executes the highest number of correct tackles within a given time (for example, 2 minutes) wins. Besides tackling, the participants learn to shield the ball, placing the body between ball and defender, to execute dummies, and to lift the head during the dribble.

7. Pressing Defense 1 on 1

Group the players in pairs, one with and the other one without a ball, and mark off a square 15 meters per side. Three pairs start the competition within this square. The tacklers try to push their attackers' balls out of the square as quickly as possible.

15 m.

VARIATION

➤ You can involve eight players in this game, having the four defenders start from outside the square once you give a visual signal. They may follow any attacker—or you may set it up so that they may tackle only one particular (their personal) attacker. The defender who last clears a ball out of the square is the loser.

8. The Cage

Group the youngsters in sets of five and set up several 10-meter squares. Four of the players are attackers positioned outside the square, each with a ball. To score a point, each of the four attackers must manage to run with the ball under control through the square. The defender remains inside the square throughout the game. Call on the attackers, one after another, until they all have attacked twice. After the player inside the square has defended 1 on 1 for these eight times, players switch positions until everyone has been a defender. The player who allows fewest goals to be scored wins. As teacher or coach, you should educate the attackers waiting their turn on the sidelines around the square to spot any mistakes on the part of the defender.

9. Substitutes and 1 on 1

Set up a playing field 12 meters wide by 20 meters long, with goals marked by the cones at the ends. Have two youngsters stationed within the field and two waiting beyond the goals on the ends of the field. The two players within the playing area face each other until one of them is able to control the ball into the opposing goal area (12 meters wide) on the end line. After a goal is scored or after the ball has run across any goal line, both attackers must return to their respective goal (to rest). Meanwhile, the two substitutes step in from behind their respective goal areas and continue the game. The practice is over when one team (or one player) manages to score six goals.

Besides assuming a correct basic position for tackling (with the legs well bent), the defender must learn to position his or her body so that the right shoulder is opposite the attacker's right shoulder. This position enables the player to channel the attacker to his right and, usually, strong foot. As coach, you should encourage him to execute dummies and to switch immediately to attack after having gained complete control over the ball. Depending on the attacker's speed and technical ability, the defender learns to use different tackling techniques.

10. Game With Four Goals

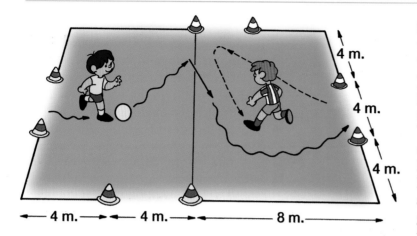

Set up a playing field as shown in the illustration, with cones set out to leave 4-meter gaps. Have two youngsters at a time play in each playing area; there should be a soccer ball for each pair that plays. They try to dribble the ball through one of two wide goals set up to the left (or right) and opposite him or her at the other end of the playing area. The coach assigns the two goals. The player without the ball tries to defend these two goals, that is, the goal behind and the other one to the right (or left) side.

When the attacker starts the game, the defender in the opposite goal area should react immediately, leaving the goal and trying to prevent the opponent from scoring in either of the two goals you assigned him or her. If the ball runs out of the playing area or if a goal is scored, the game resumes, but with the players switching roles.

After an infringement, the attacker is awarded a free dribble—with the defender no closer than 2 meters' distance. The defender may interfere only after the attacker resumes play. The winner is the player who scores the most goals in 10 attempts.

Before putting this game to the test, have the two players experiment in tag games on the same field without using a ball. They should practice trying out the rules, how to get away from the opponent, the use of dummies, the art of channeling, and employing a sudden change of direction and speed.

11. 1 on 1 for Mini-Soccer

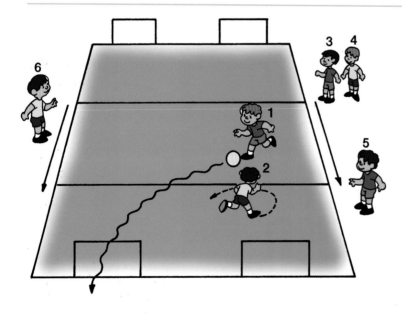

Use a mini-soccer field that is 20 to 25 meters by 35 to 40 meters, with pairs of goals set up on either end. Six children participate, forming three pairs to practice the 1-on-1 situation. The game is started with a ball toss in the center of the field. The object is to prevent the opponent from dribbling the ball through either of the team's two goals. Once the defense is successful, a counter-attack is launched, with the former attacker tackling back. In order to encourage a defender to channel an attacker deliberately to the right or left side, you (as coach) may award fewer points for scoring a goal on the defender's right-hand side than for scoring a goal on the left-hand side (or vice versa).

Level-1 Competitions

Decathlon and 2-on-2 Triathlon competitions should be organized periodically as part of the training program for beginners. At Level 1 youngsters are not yet ready to compete with other clubs or institutions, which might create unnecessarily stressful situations.

Soccer Decathlon

The Soccer Decathlon is a simplified competition for beginners. You can also use it as a test to establish the performance level of each player compared with his or her peers. The decathlon ensures that young players encounter the most important soccer fundamentals in real-game situations—how to execute a skill well is as important as when and where to play the ball.

The following ten activities have been pulled from "Games for Basic Abilities and Capacities," described earlier, to form a decathlon.

1. The Tunnel

See Dribbling Games, No. 2, for game description.

TRAINING OBJECTIVES

- To pass the ball with correct speed through the open legs of an opponent and to recover it as quickly as possible.
- To use both feet to save time.
- To improve footwork and keep the center of gravity relatively low to enhance quick changes of directions.

2. Dribbling Maze Game

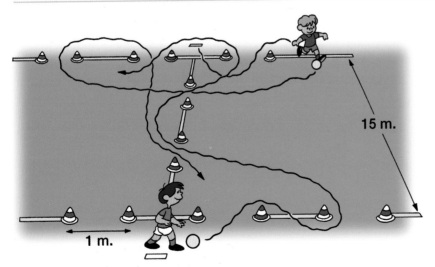

15 m.

1 m.

See Games in the Maze, No. 1, for game description.

TRAINING OBJECTIVES

- To dribble the ball according to the position of the goals with the inside or outside of the right or left foot.
- To learn to collect information by raising the view (head and eyes) frequently while dribbling.

- To change the direction of the dribble.
- To find the shortest route; to mentally anticipate the next action.

3. Passing and Receiving 1 on 1

See Passing, Receiving, and Shooting Games, No. 7, for game description.

TRAINING OBJECTIVES

- To execute passes along the ground with different techniques.
- To know how to disguise the direction of the pass.
- To receive or save the ball in a correct basic position with the legs sufficiently bent.
- To receive the ball, in motion, with either foot.
- To anticipate or read the direction of the opponent's pass.
- To enlarge the range of action of the defender.

4. Hot Pursuit

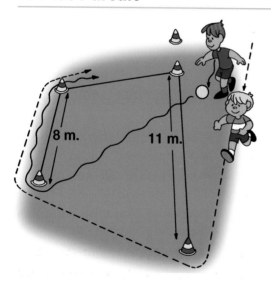

See Dribbling Games, No. 19, for game description.

TRAINING OBJECTIVES

- To dribble the ball at high speed without losing control despite several changes of direction.
- To use the appropriate dribble technique when carrying the ball on a straight line and when changing its direction.
- To use the appropriate running technique when changing direction. After having lowered the center of gravity, the body's weight, which rests on one leg, must be pushed with a full extension of the same leg into the new direction. At the same time, the ball is played with the other foot.
- During the dribble, to protect the ball with the body when the defender is close.

5. The Tackle

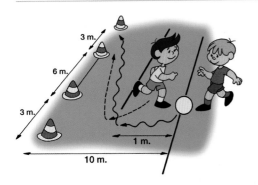

See Tackling Games, No. 3, for game description.

TRAINING OBJECTIVES

- To assume an optimal basic position before executing the tackle.
- To know the importance of executing a tackle with the elements of speed and surprise.
- To execute a dummy move before stepping in.
- To anticipate the opponent's play, that is, the direction in which he is moving the ball.
- To recover the basic tackling position quickly in order to tackle a second or third time.
- As attacker, to attentively observe the preparation and execution of the opponent's tackle so as to move the ball out of that player's range of action.
- To learn to tackle at the right instant, especially when the ball is not close to the attacker's feet.

6. The Challenge

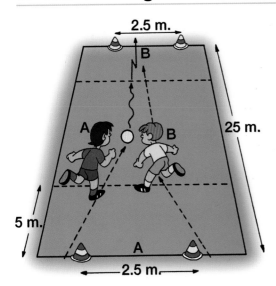

See Dribbling Games, No. 25, for game description.

TRAINING OBJECTIVES

- To run to the ball quickly and try to gain the best position to play it first.
- To dribble and keep possession of the ball against an opponent defending from behind.
- To defend from a sideways position, not from behind, in relation to the attacker.
- To score despite the presence of an opponent.
- To change quickly from attack to defense and vice versa.
- To execute a precise pass from 12.5 meters when a penalty is awarded to the attacker.
- To avoid dribbling the ball into the range of the defender.

7. Quick Goals

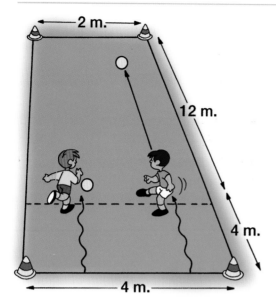

See Passing, Receiving, and Shooting Games, No. 6, for game description.

TRAINING OBJECTIVES

- To accelerate with a ball from a stationary position.
- To combine two basic technical moves, such as dribbling the ball in front of the body and executing a pass or shot quickly.
- To execute the pass not only quickly and accurately but also with explosive power so that the ball travels through the goal first.
- To position the support leg correctly level with the ball to assure accuracy.

8. Putting the "Wrong" Foot Forward

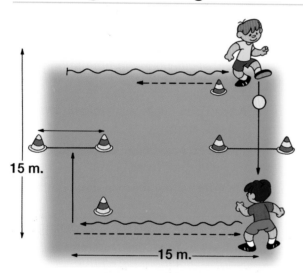

See Passing, Receiving, and Shooting Games, No. 14, for game description.

TRAINING OBJECTIVES

- To ensure accuracy when passing with the less-skillful foot.
- While preparing the pass, to avoid giving away information about its moment of execution and direction.

9. Head Kick Into the Goal

See Passing, Receiving, and Shooting Games, No. 22, for game description.

TRAINING OBJECTIVES

- To give a first experience with headers.
- To motivate young players to train with several progressive exercises getting out of a sitting and kneeling position.
- To execute headers in a technically correct way in a stationary, standing position.

10. Game With Four Goals

See Tackling Games, No. 10, for game description.

TRAINING OBJECTIVES

- While dribbling the ball, to raise the eyes to observe and analyze the opponent's position and play.
- To avoid dribbling the ball into the range of the defender.
- By dribbling the ball to one side, to force the defender to move in that direction; then to enter the space thus created with a sudden change of speed and direction.
- To improve the dribble technique with a change of speed and direction.
- For defenders to learn to force the attacker to dribble the ball into a desired space.
- For defenders to learn to use dummies while defending.

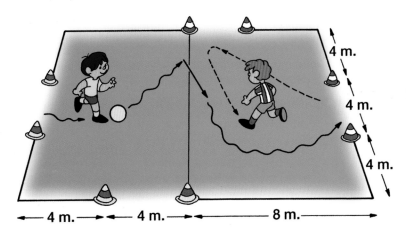

Organizing the Decathlon

There are various possibilities for organizing a decathlon competition. Two of the best options are to structure the decathlon as either a 2-day or 10-day competition.

Two-day competition: an unlimited number of participants run through five tests each day. You can organize the games so that the decathlon is an individual competition or a team competition.

To create an individual competition, choose between these options:

1. In each test a player meets a different opponent. Players draw lots to choose the pairings for each of the 10 tests. The winner of the decathlon challenge is the player who wins the most tests. If there is a draw, use Test 10 or Test 2 as a tie-breaker.

2. In each test a player meets the same opponent. The coach ensures that two players of very similar technical, tactical, and physical level face each other in all 10 tests. The winner is the player who wins the most tests against his personal opponent.

In a team competition, two teams (clubs or schools) compete, both with the same number of players. In each event, a player from one team meets a player from the other team, changing opponents for each of the 10 tests. The winning team is the one that wins the most tests.

Ten-day competition: only one of the 10 tests will be organized during each training session, and the winner will be sought from among all the participants. If there are fewer than 7 participants, have them all compete against each other until the winner is established. If there are between 8 and 14 participants, divide them into two groups, the winners of which meet in the final. If there are 16 or more players, a knockout tournament is organized, and both the winners and the losers play their final rounds.

Introducing Each Event

To introduce one of the 10 tests in the training session for the beginners do the following:

1. First prepare the playing area and select two players for demonstration. Then explain the rules of the game (test), slowly demonstrating how the game develops. Ask several questions to be sure the players understand the rules and everybody knows how to win the test. Finally, a full demonstration of the test takes place.

2. Give all players the opportunity to practice with a chosen partner for 3 to 5 minutes to gain experience in the game (test).

3. After the practice, the beginners should explain in a short dialogue with you their first experiences for winning the test.

4. As coach, you should select who is playing against whom and where (what playing area) their first competition will occur.

5. The first competition takes place.

6. Discuss why one player won and the other lost the first game or test. Discover together the reasons for the win or loss.

7. Use a couple corrective exercises to isolate an important aspect of the test that adversely affected the performance of the players. Then help the children practice that aspect.

8. Second competition takes place (the winners play against the winners, and the losers play the consolation round).

9. Together with the young players, work out the necessary skills and capacities to win the test. The aim is for all players to have a complete understanding of what to do at every moment while undergoing the competition test. That is why one or two more corrective exercises should be practiced to help to overcome any deficiencies observed in the beginners. Sometimes taking one step backward can be the best way to advance.

10. Third competition takes place to establish the most skillful players in this test of the decathlon.

2-on-2 Triathlon

The triathlon competition focuses on different basic, collective situations of the soccer game. Players experiment not only with how to pass, dribble, receive, or tackle but also with when, where, and why to do it, always considering the play of another teammate as well as one or two defenders. By practicing the three simplified games here, players learn to read the situations and react accordingly, despite the increasing complexity of the games.

The following figure shows how a triathlon competition can be organized. In this example the different teams designated as Europe compete against the teams designated as Africa until a winner is decided. You can use the blank spaces next to each triathlon game to record scores.

Europe against Africa

Teams	Italy	Germany	Spain	England
Names of players				

Teams	South Africa	Ghana	Nigeria	Cameron
Names of players				

First game: 2-on-1 with counterattack (4 × 2 min.)

Scores

ITA-GHA		
GER-SA		
SP-CMR		
ENG-NGR		

Second game: 2-on-2 with four intersecting goals (3 × 3 min.)

Scores

ITA-SA		
GER-GHA		
SP-NGR		
ENG-CMR		

Third game: 2-on-2 on with two wide goals (3 × 3 min.)

Scores

ITA-CMR		
GER-NGR		
SP-SA		
ENG-GHA		

Final result: Europe against Africa _____ _____

Technical delegate: _____

Note: During the triathlon, changing the composition of the team is not permitted.

Organization of the 2-on-2 triathlon.

1. 2 on 1 With Counterattack

Two players alternately attack two goals, each defended by one opponent. After a successful defense, the ball is passed by the opponent to the other defender at the opposite goal, who tries to score. After having lost the ball, the attackers should tackle back to their own half of the playing area. To score, a player must dribble the ball across the opponent's goal line. After 2 minutes, switch the attackers with the defenders. Free kicks or dribbles should be executed no less than 3 meters from the end line or centerline.

Playing time: 4 times, 2 minutes each trial, for 8 minutes.

2. 2 on 2 With Four Intersecting Goals

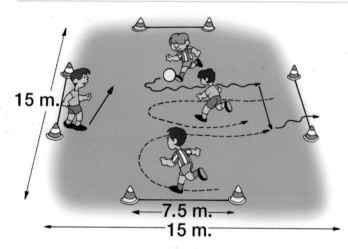

The field should have four goal areas, each 7.5 meters wide. Each team attacks the two goals assigned to it and defends the other two. The game starts with a ball toss. Free kicks and free dribbles should be executed no less than 3 meters away from the goal lines. To score, the ball has to be dribbled across one of the opposing goals.

Playing time: three times, 3 minutes each trial, with 1 minute's rest between trials.

3. 2 on 2 With Two Wide Goals

Set up the field to be 15 meters in length and the goal cones to be 12 meters (width) apart. The game starts with a ball toss. Free kicks or free dribbles should be taken from no less than 3 meters' distance from the goal line. To score, the player must have the ball under control in the opponents' goal area.

Playing time: three trials of 3 minutes, with rest intervals of 1 minute between trials.

The basic game situations of Level 1 provide children with a solid foundation. Having played and practiced these games, the young players have had adequate stimuli to make their training both effective and enjoyable: they are starting out on the right foot. Coaches can continue to build on this foundation by exposing their players to the simplified games in the next chapter—Level 2.

4

Games for Mini-Soccer
Level 2

The game of soccer doesn't progress through an accumulation of many championships or tournaments, but through a continuous development of original ideas.

During a soccer game players face a succession of more than a hundred problems that they must solve as best they can. They must correctly observe and analyze each particular game situation to make wise decisions about these problems. Once the decision is taken, they must quickly carry out the appropriate technique without any loss of time. The speed in the decision-making process and in the execution of the skill frequently distinguishes skilled players from less talented or capable ones.

Spectators and journalists often explain the poor performance of soccer players by pointing to a lack of experience. Too often, this missing experience is because the players have not been given sufficient opportunities in the learning process to read the game and respond to different game situations. Furthermore, in the beginning years of soccer many young players have faced competitions that were too complex and didn't allow them to gain valuable experience. *A coach too often forgets in training sessions that soccer is played against opponents and, to a large extent, those opponents condition the players' next moves.*

The traditional methods of using repetitive practices of passing, receiving, or shooting drills that don't involve any opposition players have failed to take into account the contextual and cognitive nature of the game. They have tended to coach mainly "how to do it" and neglected "when to" and "why" do it. Instead of spending excessive practice time on controlling, passing, or recovering the ball, coaches should dedicate at least half of the time to understanding the game. It's essential to choose, especially when working with youths older than 10 years of age, methods that don't give priority to technique! Instead of copying and obeying the instructions of the coach, players should learn to understand, then solve on their own the different problems in the context of a simplified game.

Unfortunately, the decision making all too often remains with the coach, who continues to confront young players with typical practices that don't demand an active participation of the right hemisphere of the brain (Thorpe, Bunker, Almond 1988).

The genuine coach generates ideas and opens the mind of his players. His far-reaching task is to let the others think, instead of thinking for them.

Instead of continuing to concentrate on predictable practices, which doesn't help the players learn to cope with the unpredictability of game play, youth coaches should present the game to children as early as possible in order to allow them to enjoy and understand it. They will thereby stimulate such important capacities as vision, creativity, imagination, decision making, and anticipation. Acquiring these and other important playing capacities doesn't come from practicing just isolated skills, but through also participating in simple game situations in which players can learn to respond to the cognitive and physical demands of the game. The coach continuously modifies the rules and the conditions of the simplified game to ensure that all players gain an insight into the game they play. Assuredly, the simplified game preserves the contextual nature of the full game, but without placing too great a technical demand on players still in the early stage of their playing careers.

The following table reveals the advantages and disadvantages of using the analytical method of coaching (concentrating on technique) or the global method of coaching (focusing on real game situations). It is clear that for success both methods must be used in balance.

Analytical Versus Global Method

	Analytical method	Global method
Characteristics	Presents one isolated aspect of the game that mainly considers the execution of a technique.	Simulates situations of the real game that are determined by the play of the opponents, the teammates, and the ball carrier.
Advantages	The coach has no difficulty in improving the few aspects that are fundamental to performance of the task. Training this way achieves quick, satisfactory results. It's easy to repeat the same situation again and again until success is assured.	The coach focuses not only on technical aspects but also on tactical, physical, and mental aspects. It takes time to achieve good performance levels.
Disadvantages	An analytic exercise emphasizes only one important aspect of the game or one skill at a time. Although improvement is achieved in this particular aspect of the game or skill, it doesn't guarantee overall development.	Mastery of the fundamental skills is often neglected.
Motivation	In relation to the global method, players show lower levels of motivation.	Because of the total involvement of the young player in the activity, a high level of motivation is observed.
Capacities that affect play	*Capacities of perception:* The training situations, little modified, demand little input from the pupils.	*Capacities of perception:* Teammates and opponents often face unpredictable situations. Therefore the demands on perception are far greater than those when using the analytical method.
	Capacities of decision making: As the tasks are already fixed and known in advance, the players are not asked to make decisions.	*Capacities of decision making:* Following the great variety of different stimuli or problems perceived, the player must first understand and then resolve them as quickly and as efficiently as possible.
	Capacities of skill execution: By concentrating on only one isolated skill, the players quickly learn to execute it, but without knowing where, when, and why to use it.	*Capacities of skill execution:* With the many aspects, less emphasis is put on skill improvement in a game.

The conclusion: Both methods have to be used in training and both are considered valid so long as they are used in balance.

What Are Simplified Games?

Understanding the complex game of soccer can be best achieved through the practice of a logical progression of simplified games, with a gradual increase in the numbers of players on the teams. Just as young players are growing physically and mentally, the difficulty and complexity of the simplified games are growing as well.

The games in this chapter are called "simplified" because they have these characteristics:

➤ Reduced number of participants

➤ Reduced dimensions of the playing field

➤ Simplified rules that are flexible and adaptable to the existing conditions

➤ Limited numbers of game situations

➤ Simplification of the problems

➤ Easier contexts for coaches to be able to observe, analyze, evaluate, and correct the performance of all players in the game

These qualities that characterize the simplified games in this book will have a positive impact on both coaches and players for several reasons, including these:

➤ Exposing children to simplified games with teams of only two, three, or four players leads to far fewer technical and tactical errors when later competing in more complex games (7-on-7 or 8-on-8 soccer).

➤ Frequent execution of the same techniques stimulates the acquisition and perfection of skills, as does having less distraction by many other teammates and opponents. Moreover, with fewer players, there is more time and space available, facilitating correct execution of techniques.

➤ To become a good soccer player, a child must learn to perceive the current game situation: the position of the ball, teammates and opponents on the move, location of the goals, and lines on the field. The simplified games not only aid the progressive development of perception but also enable young players to analyze game situations and make correct decisions.

➤ The frequent appearance of the same basic game situations allows players to experiment with different solutions until they are able to resolve on their own the problems presented in the simplified game. Later, when the same or similar game situation reappears in a more complex competition, the player is likely to recognize it and instantly recall a good solution.

➤ The reduced number of players allows less-skilled youngsters to become intensively involved in the game.

➤ Because each team consists of just two to four players, the simplified games progressively develop the capacities of communication and cooperation between players.

➤ No premature specialization for any playing position occurs; the simplified games make every player play defense as well as offense or attack, on the right and on the left as well as in the center of the field. *Simplified games help develop complete and intelligent soccer players.*

Children don't need a high level of ability and capacity or specific soccer knowledge to enjoy training and competing with simplified games. The simplicity of the game itself immediately attracts young players and encourages them to resolve the problems they find in it. After a certain amount of practice, if the coach observes a deficiency (technical or tactical) that is limiting the children's playing capacity, he or she interrupts the game, isolates the problem aspect, and presents the children with corrective activities or exercises. The goal is to overcome the deficiency discovered in the global game.

For the children, practice appears in a completely different light. Instead of simply working on a skill that the coach has predetermined, the child—having discovered that he or she still lacks something to win the simplified game—is motivated to learn a particular skill determined from the context of the game. The youngster *wants* to master it to a certain degree. So the mastering of a skill is perceived not so much a prerequisite for playing a game but as a complementary part of it; the training has the clear purpose of raising the level of performance in the game in order to win it. This way drill practice does not "kill" the enthusiasm of the young players whose main wish is always to play, and also win games, rather than mastering a determined skill. *By using simplified games, a bridge is built between the learning of a new skill and its application in a complex game situation.*

Here's a procedure to follow at a training session for introducing a simplified game to your players:

Simplified games contain a reduced number of players, which allows each child to play an intensive role in the game.

1. Decide on a problem or topic to be investigated (e.g., keeping possession of the ball through passes or running toward the ball when receiving).

2. Set up an appropriate simplified game to provide the context for exploration and development of the topic.

3. Demonstrate the game with the players as you explain the rules step by step.

4. Give all the players several minutes for practice during which you check whether everybody understands the rules.

5. Set up an appropriate competition for all of the teams.

6. Observe and analyze how they play.

7. Investigate, through frequent effective questioning of all players, the tactical problems and solutions. (See "Effective Questioning" on page 80.)

8. In order to overcome the deficiencies you discover in observing the game and to convert these into correct habits, present two or three corrective exercises that all teams carry out on their competition fields. These are mainly the "Dribbling Games," "Tackling Games," and "Games for Passing, Receiving, and Shooting" of chapter 3.

9. When the game resumes, once again observe the level of play.

10. Intervene to further develop understanding (demonstrations are often necessary) and present more questions or corrective exercises (games).

11. Again observe critically the development of the play and evaluate the final performance.

Effective Questioning

Coaching is an interaction between the coach and the players. The teaching and learning process, therefore, is a dialogue rather than a monologue. To enhance performance, develop this dialogue to recognize, value, and utilize the attributes and experience of the players. Questioning demands a commitment from the coach to experiment—because most people have a natural inclination to simply tell! While most of the young players live in an environment dominated by telling, when you coach youth soccer players, you help them much more by trying to involve them in the decision-making process during the practice of simplified games; ask them to apply their knowledge and experience.

Once effective questioning is skillfully employed, it allows many game situations (previously approached through telling or instructing) to be tackled differently and, ultimately, more effectively. These are some suggestions to introduce more questioning in training:

- Develop your own sound knowledge of the simplified game and all its objectives.
- Use as few "closed" questions as possible. Open questions demand information, whereas closed questions merely call for "yes" or "no" answers.
- Start most of the questions with "What?" "When?" "Where?" or "How much?"
- Ask questions that follow the interests of the player.
- Ask follow-up questions after listening to the different answers.

Here are examples of questions for the first simplified game, "2 on 1 With Two Wide Goals:"

- When does the ideal moment arise for passing the ball? Explain!
- When should the ball carrier *not* pass the ball?
- What is the disadvantage of an early pass? Why?
- Where, ideally, should the teammate receive the ball (in relation to the defender)?
- What is your opinion about the distance between the ball carrier and the receiver? Explain your opinion to us with more detail.
- Describe the target of your pass to the teammate.
- What is the outcome if the pass is directed straight into the teammate's feet?
- What happens when the ball arrives behind the target?
- What happens to the target when both attackers move forward?
- What happens when the defender delays his tackle and retreats?
- How does the speed of the pass influence the situation?
- Is it true that the pass has to be faster the closer the ball carrier gets to the defender? Why?
- What is the most natural attacking move to be carried out by the ball carrier?
- How might the technique of the pass vary as the ball carrier gets closer to the defender before passing?
- How would the defender like the attacker to play?

In the same way, you should ask numerous questions about the defense. Coaches are encouraged to revise or adapt these sample questions to the other simplified games.

Simplified Games for 2 on 2

The simplified game situations in this chapter should be included as part of the young players' training to stimulate and help develop their decision-making capacities.

1st Simplified Game

2 on 1 With Two Wide Goals

Despite the game's title, four players participate. Two players with a ball, situated in the center of the playing area, alternately attack the 12-meters-wide goals, each defended by one opponent only. The objective of the attacker is to dribble the ball across the opposing goal line despite the opponent's active defense of it.

The attack toward one goal finishes when

- the defender has touched the ball three times,
- one of the attackers has managed to dribble the ball across the goal line,
- one attacker infringes the rules, or
- the ball runs across any end line.

In case of an infringement of the rules by the defender, a "free" attack is awarded to the attacking pair. The free attack can be started with a pass or a dribble, with the defender staying no closer than 5 meters. There is no side-out or offside.

After 10 attacks (5 toward each goal) or 90 seconds of attacking, both teams switch roles and positions. The pair that scores more goals wins. In case of a draw, a tiebreaker takes place with only two attacks for each team.

VARIATION

➤ Use the same rules, except increase the number of players to six. The goals may become less wide as well (see illustration on page 82). Two players attack one goal, which is defended by an opponent whose teammate waits behind the goal without any rights to defend. The positions and roles of the two attackers and defenders are reversed as soon as a goal is scored (the ball must be dribbled across the goal line), the ball runs behind any end line, or the defender wins the ball (after three consecutive ball touches). A third pair of players positions itself with one youngster in front and the other behind the opposite goal. The team that scores more goals in 4 minutes of play wins.

You can use other options to determine the winner:

- The team that manages to score with a dribble continues to alternately attack the two wide goals.

- The team that scores more goals in a row within a playing time of 5 minutes is the winner.

TRAINING OBJECTIVES

- Lift your head while dribbling to be able to see and analyze the game situations.
- Dribble the ball using different techniques.
- Know when to pass and when to dribble.
- Try dribbling past the defender after having carried out a dummy pass to the left or right.
- Pass the ball on the run toward the right or left.
- Wait for the best instant to pass (not too early and not too late) without penetrating in the range of action of the defender.
- Communicate with your teammate before passing.
- Pass the ball with speed and accuracy.
- Adapt to the behavior of the teammate.
- Receive the ball from either side while you are on the run.
- Look for a correct positioning before receiving the ball.
- Execute a tackle with speed and surprise.
- Select the best instant to tackle and know how to delay it.
- Simulate a tackle with a move of the body weight toward the ball.

Modifying the Rules

As you coach a simplified game, it's sometimes good to change one or even two of the given rules slightly—once the players have gained experience in the practice and in the competition of the original game. The modification of any rule will undoubtedly vary the possible responses of the players, technically, tactically, or physically. Coaches should have the capacity to modify the rules of any activity depending what their intentions are in following up on the changes.

These 10 modifications of rules might be applied to the first simplified game:

1. Every team disposes of 10 attacks without time limits.

   Training objective: to understand what to do in attack as well as in defense.

2. The attacks use only 90 seconds of the playing time.

   Training objective: to gain more experience in all positions.

3. The right attacker may execute only one pass to the left or dribble past the defender after a dummy pass.

   Training objective: to be able to overcome the defender with a single action (a pass or a dodge with or without preceding dummy pass).

4. The left attacker may choose between a pass to the right or a dodge.

   Training objective: to know the most efficient way to resolve the 2-on-1 situation.

5. A goal is considered valid only when the last control of the ball was executed on the run.

   Training objective: to receive and control the ball on the run.

6. Every team uses 20 seconds for attacking both goals as often as possible with a recovery of 2 minutes before a new attempt is launched. Every team has four chances to score a maximum number of goals.

   Training objective: to launch quick attacks.

7. Both attackers must also use both the more- and the less-skillful foot.

   Training objective: to stimulate the play with the less-skillful foot.

8. During the development of the attacks, both forwards must switch positions.

   Training objective: to use the switch systematically.

9. Both defenders may tackle in any part of the playing area. The attackers start from the center and may score in either goal area. Attackers and defenders switch functions after 10 attacks.

   Training objective: to create an intentional 2-on-1 situation.

10. Each team attacks and defends two 1-meter-wide cone goals. To score, a player must control the ball inside one of the opponent's two goals, set 12 meters away from each other.

    Training objective: to ascertain the width in attack.

By asking the attackers to score with a shot into a regular goal, after they have learned to control the ball in the widely set goal areas, the attackers will gain additionally experience in the conclusion of their attacks.

- Tackle in a side-on position and look out for the 1-on-1 situation.
- Anticipate the attacker's play, considering both the position of the player without the ball and the dribbling technique of the ball carrier.

To improve the youngsters' understanding and learning, the functions of attacking and defending are separated in this first simplified game. Depending on the level of the players, the width of the goal may have to be made wider or narrower. Once the attackers are able to score 7 or more times in 10 attacks, a more difficult and complex game or problem should be presented to them (see the following simplified games). After introducing the game, it's good to organize a practice of at least 5 minutes, thus allowing the players to face some of the game's potential problems without experiencing competitive pressure.

After the children have practiced one simplified game sufficiently, that activity may serve in one of the following training sessions as an internal competition in which several teams play, somewhat like a tennis tournament with the knockout system. The winners of the first matches advance to the winners' round; the group of losers determine the winners among them in a consolation tournament.

CORRECTIVE EXERCISES

It is important to wisely select and apply one or two corrective exercises or games after youngsters compete in the simplified game. Learning, consolidating, and perfecting at least some technical, tactical, or physical aspects of a simplified game is best accomplished by training outside of the context of the global game—and with the help of various specific corrective activities. It is not enough that a coach diagnose what the players did wrong. The coach must find the roots of the players' problems and apply appropriate remedies as soon as possible (almost immediately) after the error or problem occurs. With systematic and repetitive application of corrective activities (always right after the competition in a simplified game), the coach can transform the player's spontaneous or natural behavior (often not the correct or most efficient one) into a better one (usually similar to those seen in the adult game). An example for the game "2 on 1 With Two Wide Goals" is presented on page 85.

Every corrective exercise or game, which any coach may easily invent or choose from the "Games for Basic Abilities and Capacities," is designed to improve only one or two aspects of the game, aspects that have marred or negatively conditioned the performance of the four players in the previous competition. Consider every simplified game with its specific program of corrective exercises or games as a teaching unit. You can look on the whole program of simplified games for two-player teams as a full season's program, adding only one of the variations in a single training session.

2nd Simplified Game
2 on 1 With Counterattack

Set up two wide goals (about 6 to 8 meters in width and about 15 meters away from each other) for each field. Divide the children into two-player teams. Each play lasts 3 minutes, during which two players of one team alternately attack the goals opposite each other. Each goal is defended by one opponent only. To score, one of the two attackers has to dribble (control) the ball across the goal line. The attack is concluded when

Altering Spontaneous Reactions Through Corrective Exercises

Spontaneous, natural, and incorrect behavior in "2 on 1 With Two Wide Goals"	Improved and correct behavior in "2 on 1 With Two Wide Goals"
The attacker without the ball is situated too close to the ball carrier.	The attacker without the ball stays as "wide as possible" to make the defense more difficult.
Beginners only: The attacker without the ball is situated in front of the ball, leading the ball carrier to play a diagonal pass that is easy to intercept.	The attacker without the ball generally should stay behind the ball to discourage the ball carrier's passing of the ball through the range of action of the defender.
The attacker without the ball receives it in a stationary position and enables the defender to face and channel him.	The attacker without the ball must receive the ball while running at full speed in order to make optimal use of the space in front of him.
The direction of the pass determines where the receiver runs.	The position of the receiver always determines the direction of the pass.
The pass is directed into the feet of the receiver.	Before passing, the receiver's next moves should be anticipated (pass into the run of the receiver).
The moment of the pass is not precise: passing the ball too early or too late results in the loss of possession.	It's important to select the best moment to pass; know when to pass and when to dribble.
The attack develops too slowly.	In the shortest time possible, the two attackers should profit from their supremacy of numbers (2 against 1).
The attacker with the ball indicates the direction of the pass.	The attacker must learn not to indicate the direction of the pass.
The pass doesn't have sufficient speed.	The ball should be passed with maximal speed to allow the defense less time to intercept.
The attackers need more than one pass to play out the defender.	Both attackers should play out the defender with the least possible number of actions (one pass or one penetration only).
In most of the attacks, the right attacker is in possession of the ball.	Usually it's easier to play out the defender when the left attacker possesses the ball.
The defender runs toward the attacker who has the ball under control.	The defender should close down the attacker in possession of the ball without carrying out a fast tackle.
The defender tackles in a frontal position (shoulder parallel to the goal line).	To influence the attacker and execute more than one tackle the defender should assume a side position.
The defender remains on the goal line, leaving all initiative to the attacker.	The defender should act and not react to the attacker's moves.
The defender precipitates his tackle and doesn't execute any dummy.	The defender should carry out dummies to distract the attacker.
The defender doesn't position himself between the two attackers to engage the ball carrier in a 1-on-1 situation.	The defender should create a 1-on-1 situation, using an optimal positional play and dummies.

- a goal is scored,

- a defender (who has managed to gain possession of the ball) passes toward his teammate in the opposite goal (after receiving the ball, he should dribble it into "his" goal), or

- there is an infringement by the attackers (after an infringement, a free kick is awarded to the defender, whose task is to pass the ball to his outlet player in the opposite goal).

After an infringement by a defender, the attackers choose between a pass to the teammate or a penetration dribble (in the event that his partner is marked closely). Independent of the result of the counterattack, the next 2 on 1 should be directed toward the opposite wide goal.

The duration of the game is two attacking and two defending periods of 3 minutes for each team.

6-8 m.

15 m.

TRAINING OBJECTIVES

- To look up during the dribble to be able to observe and analyze the game situation and make correct decisions.

- To pass the ball with either foot to the left and right accurately and with sufficient speed.

- To select the best moment for the pass.

- To understand whether it is more effective to pass or dribble into a less defended area.

- To execute dummies, then suddenly accelerate and dribble past the surprised defender.

- To receive and control the ball on the run and to avoid receptions and controls while stationary.

- To always be available for a pass, adapting to the play of the ball carrier.

- To execute a tackle in a side position both correctly and quickly.

- To adapt the tackle technique (frontal tackle, sliding tackle, tackle in a side position, or tackle in retreat) to the game situation; to know which technique is the most efficient one.

- As defender, to read and anticipate the opponent's play.
- Through maintaining a correct position in relation to the ball carrier, to force that player to do what you want him or her to do.
- As defender, to use dummies to distract the opponent.
- To ensure a quick transition from playing defense to attack and vice versa; to execute a free kick as quickly as possible without indicating the trajectory of the pass.

CORRECTIVE EXERCISES

Between the simplified game competitions, perform corrective exercises or games to focus on improving one particular skill which conditions the result of the game.

3rd Simplified Game
2 on 2 With Four Intersecting Goals

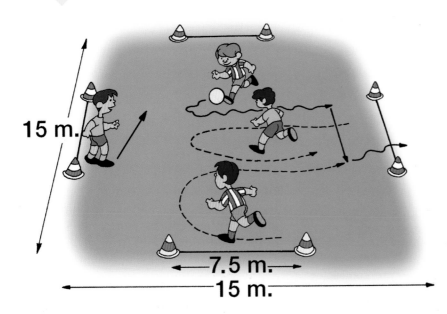

Set up four goals that are 7.5 meters wide, as shown in the illustration. Each team of two players defends two opposite goals and attacks the other two. The game is started and restarted with a ball toss at the center of the 15-meter square. When the ball runs out of the playing area or a player commits an infringement, a free kick or "free dribble" is awarded to the other team—with the opponent's and the nearest goal at least 3 meters away. A goal is scored by a dribble across one of the two opposing goal lines. The game's duration should be four periods of 3 minutes each.

VARIATIONS

➤ The cones forming goal areas remain as above, but each team attacks and defends two of the goals that are side by side (rather than opposite).

➤ Using the same field setup, the goals are defined across the corner cones instead of across the linear cones (see the illustration). Players defend neighboring goals.

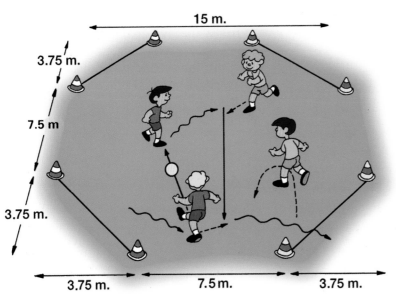

TRAINING OBJECTIVES

- To know at each moment of the game what is going on (to "read" the game) in order to make correct decisions in attacks as well as in defenses.
- To be capable of systematically creating a numerical superiority in attack by frequently changing direction and speed.
- To be aware of the less-controlled zones of the playing area and systematically use them to your advantage.
- As defender, to force the attackers to play to their counterparts.
- To consolidate the technical-tactical skills of attack and defense that players experienced in the first two simplified games.

CORRECTIVE EXERCISES

Choose and apply the corrective exercises between two competitions in the simplified game.

4th Simplified Game

2 on 1 Twice in a Game

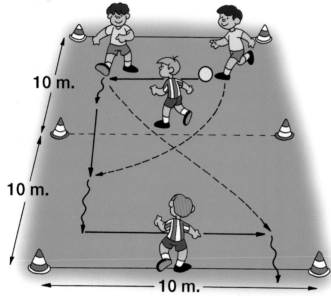

10 m.

10 m.

10 m.

For this game, set up the playing field as shown in the illustration, using six cones (having two colors of cones if possible to indicate the different end goal areas, each 10 meters wide). Designate two teams of two players each. How many times do two attackers manage to play out, one after another, the two opponents who defend individually in front of their respective goal? To score the ball must be controlled by the attackers on each end line.

Use a coin toss to decide which team starts to attack and which defends individually the two goals situated in a row. No defender may tackle behind his goal line, but the second defender may come forward of the goal when his teammate in front of him has been passed by the attackers. An attack finishes when

- two goals are scored,
- one of the two defenders manages to take the ball away from the attackers,
- the ball runs out of the playing area, or
- one of the attackers commits an infringement of the rules.

In case of an infringement of the defenders, the same rule may be applied as in the previous games.

VARIATIONS

➤ Propose a time limit for the execution of the attack.

➤ A goalkeeper may play in the position of the second defender. He must defend a goal area (set the cones only 6 meters apart, as in 7-on-7 soccer). Once the attackers manage to play out the first (or "last") defender, the goalkeeper may run out from the goal line to avoid being beaten individually with a pass to the second attacker or a shot from any distance. Choosing the most appropriate instant for running out from goal is crucial for good performance by the goalkeeper.

➤ For more advanced players: youngsters play "2 on 1" three times in front of the penalty area, with the third goal line being part of the 11-meter line of the 7-on-7 soccer field. Once all three defenders are outplayed, the two attackers practice goal scoring without any delay against a goalkeeper who defends the regular goal.

➤ Use three defenders, but only one of the defenders intervenes at a time. The first defender begins his or her tackling in front of the first goal line, and in case the initial tackle is unsuccessful, retreats to also defend the second goal (see the illustration). The second defender, meanwhile, is situated at the top of the penalty area in the third goal and intervenes after the attackers cross the second goal. The second defender covers the back area together with the third defender, who is the goalkeeper.

➤ Instead of the attackers always being on one side of the ball carrier, now the attacker without the ball positions herself behind the first defender at the start of the attack. Here, she may expect a pass or may wait for the ball carrier to join her after play with the defender in front of the first goal has succeeded. The second defender is not allowed to mark the teammate of the ball carrier; he must remain in his goal until the ball has crossed the first goal line.

TRAINING OBJECTIVES

The objectives are the same as in the first and second simplified games for 2 on 2.

CORRECTIVE EXERCISE

Apply the following corrective exercise to the fourth simplified game.

Pass or Beat the Defender

Phase 1: two players, an attacker and a defender, are situated on the goal line. Ten meters in front of the defender, a second attacker dribbles the ball toward him with the intention of beating him individually or passing the ball to her teammate on the left. With a triangular pass (direct or with not more than two ball touches), the attacker on the goal line returns the ball immediately into the run of his teammate who positions herself behind the defender. The latter, without leaving the goal line, tries to intercept the first or the return pass.

Phase 2: after completing the first attack, the second player in possession of the ball dribbles toward the goal to the former passer, beats him individually with or without a dummy—or passes the ball to his teammate on the right. Without delay the teammate returns the ball with a maximum of two touches to the attacker who collects it on the run behind the defender. After 10 attacks of both attackers, carried out alternatively from the right and left sides of the goal, the four players switch positions and functions.

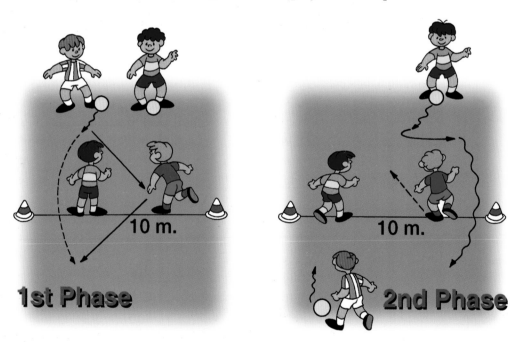

1st Phase   10 m.   **2nd Phase**   10 m.

5th Simplified Game
Through Passes to the Front Runners

The game is played on the mini-soccer field (see the illustration for the setup) with two teams formed of four players each. Two of the players must always remain in the opposing shooting zone (which is 6 meters deep), waiting for a pass from their two teammates in the midfield. After having received and controlled the ball within their shooting zone, they try to score in either goal. Once the ball enters the shooting zone, all midfield players (attackers as well as defenders) are allowed to join the two front runners. After every goal or any time the ball goes outside of the field, the former defenders restart the game from the 6-meter line with either a short pass to the teammate or a dribble, the defenders at a distance of at least 3 meters.

Duration of the game: four periods of 3 minutes, with 2 minutes' rest to work out the deficiencies. After every 3 minutes the midfield players switch positions and functions with the front runners.

25 m.

VARIATIONS

➤ To improve the reception and control of lifted balls, the attackers execute aerial passes into the shooting zones.

➤ Only those through passes that are executed with the less-skillful foot are considered valid.

➤ Only goals scored by one of the midfield players are considered valid. This rule helps all midfield players learn to support the outlet players after a successful through pass.

TRAINING OBJECTIVES:

- For players to learn that before a through pass is played, passer and receiver should connect visually.
- For players to learn that during the dribble and reception of the ball, the ball carrier should always be aware of the positions of the two teammates in the depth of the field and the support of the other midfield player.
- To execute a free kick quickly and before the opposing team has reorganized its defense. Players should understand that a through pass is preferable to a horizontal pass.
- To switch quickly from defense to attack and vice versa and to watch for the through pass immediately after having recovered the ball.
- To hide the direction of the through pass.

CORRECTIVE EXERCISES

See the last variation of the fourth simplified game (as well as the ninth simplified game, later in this chapter). Other good activities are found in the program's "Games for Receiving, Passing, and Shooting" (in chapter 3), which lists exercises for improving the accuracy and speed of the pass.

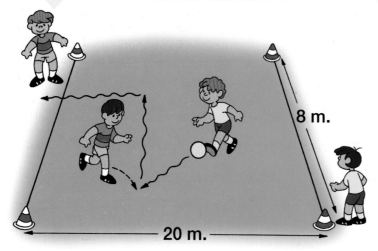

6th Simplified Game
1 on 1 With Substitutions

Two opposing players face each other in the middle of a practice field (8 meters by 20 meters) with the objective to dribble the ball through the opponent's goal. The younger player attacks first. After a goal or the ball's going beyond any end line, both players must leave the playing area and return behind their respective goals. Meanwhile, the two other players, who have so far been behind the goals, now substitute for them, entering the field for a new 1-on-1 situation with the partner of the former defender in possession of the ball. The winning team is the pair of players who first manage to dribble the ball through the opposing goal six times.

TRAINING OBJECTIVES

There are three objectives for the attackers.

- Keep the ball out of the defender's range of action and protect the ball with the body.
- Vary the play, outbalance the defender, and use speed (especially changes of speed).
- While attacking, stay alert and aware of the basic position, the positional play, and the defensive actions of your opponent.

There are three objectives for the defenders.

- Get close to the attacker, generally, with the right shoulder opposite the right one of the attacker and the left foot placed slightly in front. This position allows a defender to channel the attacker to the right side.
- Tackle with speed and aim to surprise the attacker.
- Use dummies to oblige the attacker to show his or her intention. (Also review the general recommendations or rules for tackling.)

CORRECTIVE EXERCISES

There are many activities to choose among for corrective exercise. See the "Dribbling Games," "Tackling Games," and play 1 on 1 on a mini-soccer field.

7th Simplified Game
Control the Ball and Beat Your Opponent

Set up the field as shown in the illustration, with cones set 12 meters apart to mark goal areas. The game is played between two goals at opposite ends of a field that is 10 meters long for the youngest players and 20 meters long for the more experienced ones. Behind and parallel to the goal lines you should draw a second line, 2 meters away from the first one. At the instant that Attacker A passes the ball to B, Attacker B runs quickly with Defender D toward the ball to receive and control it in front of the cone goal outside the 2-meter zone. The defender is not allowed to tackle in front of the cone goal, but tries to prevent the attacker from dribbling the ball through the 2-meter zone and across the back line. In case the attacker is successful, the attackers remain in attack and do the same play in the opposite direction. But if the defender gains possession of the ball, touching it three times consecutively, or if the ball runs out of the playing area, the defender gets to switch positions and function as an attacker. The pair that manages to score 10 goals wins. If you have more than four players, you may organize a tournament to establish the best team in passing, receiving under simplified conditions, and dribbling with an opponent.

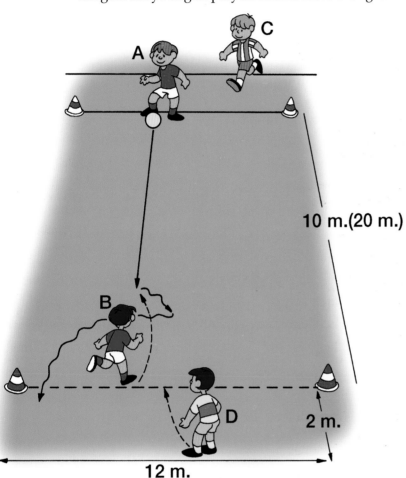

VARIATIONS

➤ Ask for aerial passes to improve the skill of receiving and controlling the ball with one or two touches. Players should know and experiment with an "oriented" or "purposeful" and planned control of the ball, anticipating during the reception their next attacking move.

➤ The defender may intervene beyond the goal line, thus reducing the attacker's time and space for controlling the ball and to try to win the point.

TRAINING OBJECTIVES:

• Perfect the communication skills between the passer and receiver.

- Learn to run to the ball, rather than waiting for it to come to your feet, to avoid the defender's anticipating your play.
- Put your body between the defender and the oncoming ball before you receive and control it.
- While beating the defender, try to force him to move to one side; then pass him on the opposite side, using a change of speed and direction.
- Execute as often as possible a control of the ball that will facilitate your next attacking move.
- As a defender, learn to not rush when the attacker manages to control the ball completely. Understand how it is better to move back some steps to help delay your tackle until the ball is a little loose and more available.
- Anticipate the opponent's play.
- Assume an optimal basic position before tackling; always place yourself in a correct line to the attacker.

CORRECTIVE EXERCISES

Choose among the tackling games in "Games for Basic Abilities and Capacities."

8th Simplified Game
Free Kick to a Marked Attacker

Four players participate: two play inside a 10-meter square and two are stationed outside, one in front and the other behind the square. Toss a coin to determine which team attacks and which defends. The attacker outside the square executes a free kick to his teammate in the center of the square, who tries to receive the ball despite the presence and defense of an opponent.

6 m.

10 m.

6 m.

For practice purposes the defender should position himself on either side of the attacker or behind him; he may not position himself in front. To avoid the defender's anticipating the opponent's play, the attacker, in the moment of executing the pass, must run toward the ball. Then the attacker tries to receive the ball, control it, and, protecting it with his body, pass it as quickly as possible through the wide goal to the third player behind the square. Player 3 now repeats the actions of the first player, passing the ball to the former defender who is closely marked by the former attacker. The attack is over when the attacker is successful (this scores one point), the ball is run out of the square, or the attacker makes a rules infringement. If the defender breaks the rules, the attackers also get a point. The team (pair of players) that first manageṣ to complete 10 correct controls with subsequent pass to the player outside the square wins. After completing the first competition, both players of both teams change positions and functions.

VARIATIONS

➤ The receiver may return the ball to the passer, who then restarts the game from any position outside the square.

➤ The passer and receiver gain 2 points if the receiver is able to deflect the oncoming ball with one touch directly into the run of the third player.

➤ Practice with only three players. After every three free kicks, the players switch positions. When the defender recovers possession of the ball, he or she is asked to return it to the passer.

TRAINING OBJECTIVES

- Learn to establish mutual agreement between the passer and receiver.
- Be able to "read" how the defender marks his opponent. In case the defender marks him from behind, the free kick should be directed into the attacker's feet; a marking from any side of the attacker requires a pass to the side uncovered by the defender.
- Improve in choosing the optimal instant to pass the ball to the receiver.
- Learn to facilitate ball control by the receiver's gaining an optimal position in relation to the defender, putting his body between him and the ball, thus protecting the ball and not allowing the defender to anticipate the attacking play.
- Learn to select the best technique for reception, depending on the successive play. The angle of the foot in relation to the direction of the oncoming ball (90, 60, or 120 degrees) will determine whether the attacker looks first for assuring possession of the ball or to continue the attack from a side-on position as quickly as possible.
- Learn to deflect oncoming balls directly to the teammate.
- Learn to delay the pass after receiving the ball in case playing it would be very risky.

CORRECTIVE EXERCISES

See the Seventh Simplified Game, "Control the Ball and Beat Your Opponent."

9th Simplified Game
Maintaining Ball Possession 2 on 1

15 m.

In this game, which actually involves four players, two players try to keep possession of the ball inside a square for as long as possible or for 15 seconds. A defender, always starting from the center of the square, does everything to prevent them from achieving their aim. His function is to play the attacker's ball out of the square while his teammate outside of the square (the fourth player) counts the seconds until the ball runs out of the square or the attackers infringe on the rules. In any of these cases, the defender inside the square switches positions and functions with the fourth player (and teammate) until both have defended five times each in this 1-on-2 situation. After 10 trials the attackers established their record time.

Next, both teams change functions. The first set of (former) defenders now have the chance to improve the result of the former attackers. Whenever a defender infringes on the rules, the time is stopped until the attackers restart the game with a pass or a dribble. If there are more than two teams, you might organize a tournament to determine which pair of players can best keep possession of the ball. Players younger than 10 years of age should play in a square that is 15 meters per side. The more advanced the players are, the smaller the playing area should be.

If you have only three players available, the attacker who loses possession of the ball three times becomes defender.

TRAINING OBJECTIVES

- Know when to pass and when to keep possession of the ball.
- Learn to continually be ready and open for a pass, to run out of the shadow of the defender, when you don't have the ball.
- While in possession of the ball keep an eye on your teammate as well as on the defender.
- Keep the ball close to the feet to be able to pass it quickly if necessary.
- Look out and make use of the zones that the defender isn't covering. Understand that the greater the distance between the passer and receiver, the more difficult is the defender's job.
- Learn to hide your intentions (the moment of the pass and its direction). Use frequently dummies or feints.
- Avoid entering the defender's range of action; learn to put your body between the ball and the defender in case no pass is possible and the defender is close.

- As defender, learn to reduce the space and time at the disposal of the attackers. Show will power until you succeed.
- Anticipate the attackers' play.
- Execute dummies to condition and direct the attacker's play.

CORRECTIVE EXERCISES

- Offer a tag game with both attackers trying to run from any direction across the playing area without getting tagged by one defender in the field's center.
- Review the first five simplified games for teams of two players.
- Review the dribbling games "Cops and Robber," "Maintaining Ball Possession," "Cat and Mouse," and "Escape."

10th Simplified Game
2 on 2 With Two Wide Goals

Start the game with a ball toss at the center of the playing area (set up as shown in the illustration with wide goal areas, 12 to 15 meters). Divide players into two teams of two players. To score a goal, an attacker must control the ball in the opponent's goal. The two cones of the goals are placed opposite each other at a distance that depends on the players' ages. Usually there are no sidelines. A rules infringement is penalized with a free kick or "free dribble" from a point at least 3 meters away from the opponents and their goal.

Duration of the game: four periods of 2 minutes each.

12 m.

15 m.

VARIATIONS

➤ The same game is played using four goals, but each only 6 meters wide (see illustration). To score, the ball must be dribbled across one of the two opponents' goals.

➤ The youngsters play the game around an open, 6-meter-wide goal area marked off by cones. The team that does not have the ball uses one of its two players as goalkeeper, and this player may not leave the goal line. But once that team manages to win or capture the ball, the goalkeeper may go off the line. After one successful pass between the defenders, they obtain the right to attack the goal from any side, with one former attacker defending it. A goal can be scored from any distance.

TRAINING OBJECTIVES

- In attack, learn to look out systematically for the 2-on-1 situation by frequently dribbling the ball straight to the other defender who marks the second attacker. When this defender turns her interest to the ball carrier, the latter passes the ball to the second attacker who stays wide and controls the ball on the run to give the defense less time to interfere.

- Learn the switch: after a diagonal penetration by the ball carrier, her teammate stays slightly back and then positions himself for a pass with a sudden run behind the ball carrier (see the illustration for the first variation of the Tenth Simplified Game).

- Review and continue to work on the coaching objectives for the previous simplified games.

Coaching Simplified Games

- Be aware of the progression in the program of the simplified games for teams of two, three, and then four players.

- Know the training or coaching objectives of every single simplified game—as well as how its grade of difficulty and complexity compares with the previous and next games in the program. This enables you as a coach to link the exercise or game with the technical-tactical experience players have gained in the previous games. And by progressing this way, the children, on their own, can resolve most of the problems contained in the game.

- Consider the players' capacity level as well as their actual mental and physical state to be able to adapt the dimensions of the playing area, the goals, and the rules to their state of development.

- Objectively face the actual playing level you find in your players with the level they should eventually achieve in their age group.

- Offer feedback and simplified games, preferably in which players learn the result of the execution of a skill immediately after their efforts and know the reasons why they failed or succeeded.

- Identify any aspects that are restricting the performance levels of the players, the causes of an error, and the necessary remedies (corrective exercises or games) to help youngsters form correct habits.

- Consider the motivation of every player and create the positive atmosphere during a training session that is essential for learning. Provide every player with sufficient opportunities to experiment with successful moves; present slightly modified situations to consolidate the new experiences players have gained.

- Always consider youngsters as *active* learners during the training session: players learn better when they are given the opportunity to resolve the problems on their own without the help of their coach or teacher.

Preparatory Games for Mini-Soccer

The preparatory or corrective games let the children experience the most important skills needed for playing mini-soccer.

1. Attack 3 on 0 (3 Players Without Defense)

Set up a mini-soccer or basketball field, with four goal areas as shown in the illustration (on page 100) and two shooting zones of 5.8 meters. Form several teams, each having three players, that will compete against each other. Each team starts its attack from one end line. Before the team members score in either goal area from inside the shooting zone, every player must have touched the ball at least once. Each team tries to score five goals with five attacks. An attack finishes when the ball leaves the field, enters the goal, or simply misses its aim.

VARIATIONS

➤ Consider a goal valid only if the three players have attacked in *a triangular formation* with a distance of at least 5 meters between them.

➤ Each player has to touch the ball at least once with his or her less-skillful foot.

➤ All receptions of the ball must be executed on the run. Controlling the ball when stationary is considered a mistake.

➤ A goal counts only when all attackers conclude the attack in a different attacking position.

➤ To win, the team must score its goal in the least time.

➤ All variations can be executed, adding a goalkeeper to defend both goals to be attacked by the three players.

To "polish off" and eliminate any deficiencies in the dribble, passing, or receiving skills, the coach should consult the exercise activities or games proposed in "Games for Basic Abilities and Capacities—Level 1" (chapter 3), allowing players ample opportunities to review and practice their developing skills.

2. Attack 3 on 1

Three attackers start with the ball from one end line of the mini-soccer field, but now they must overcome a defender before penetrating into the area to score a goal in one of the two goal areas. Here the attackers learn to

- attack with sufficient width,
- ensure that when they face the defender, the ball is with the center forward (who has the best options for passing),

- execute the pass at the right instant without coming within the reach of the opponent or revealing the direction in which the pass is going,
- execute the pass to the best-situated teammate,
- overcome the defender individually after having carried out a dummy pass, and
- attack in a triangular formation.

The team that scores the highest number of goals within five attacks is the winner. An attack concludes

- when the opponent manages to touch the ball three consecutive times,
- when the ball runs across the opposing goal line or any sideline,
- when the attackers infringe on the rules, or
- when a goal is scored.

After five attacks, the teams switch places, and one of the former attackers can be defender.

VARIATIONS

➤ After every five attacks, the defender must be substituted by a former attacker. The defender who allows fewest goals to be scored is the winner. To help improve performance, ask the attackers or the defender about the reason(s) for their (or his or her) failure or success.

➤ When the defender manages to recover the ball, he has to score a goal with a pass from any distance through one of the two opposite goals.

➤ The team needing the least time to score is winner. Question the players to lead them to work out more effective strategies or combinations for attacking.

➤ The three attackers play against one defender *and* a goalkeeper who has to defend both goals.

➤ Use three teams to play a 3-on-1 game (see illustration). The team initially situated in the center of the field alternately attacks both goals on the end lines during 2 minutes (or 10 times). After each attack the defender changes place and function with another teammate, who had been observing the last attack from a position off the field. Whichever team scores most goals is the winner.

➤ See the first variation. A second defender stands 6 to 8 meters behind the three attackers or 6 meters away from any sideline of the mini-soccer field. When the attackers start from the end line, the second defender runs into the field to help his fellow defender in the opposite shooting zone stop the attack. If the attack is carried out without speed, the 3-on-1 game turns into a 3-on-2 situation because the slower action allows the second defender into the play. The attack must be carried out with high speed to maintain the advantage.

➤ Add a goalkeeper to the last variation.

3. Attack 3 on 2

For practicing the 3-on-2 situation, repeat all the variations proposed for the previous two games (1 and 2), first without and later with a goalkeeper joining the defenders.

VARIATION

➤ This variation is a game between two teams. The team in possession of the ball alternately attacks the goals on the two end lines. These are defended on one end by two defenders (creating a 3-on-2 situation) and on the other one by a single defender (creating a 3-on-1 situation). After 10 attacks, the teams switch positions and functions.

Testing an Individual's Playing Capacity

Ordinarily, during soccer sessions, you will expose the young players to a varied program of activities, proposed in Levels 1 and 2 of the Soccer Development Model. For contrast and motivational challenge, however, as well as for your own checking of progress, pick three times during the season to organize a test of their capacity to play mini-soccer well. Before you propose the following test, group the youngsters in sets of six players and assign every boy or girl a number.

1. 1-on-1 Challenge

Player 1 challenges Player 2, Player 3 plays against Player 4, and Player 5 competes against Player 6. The game is played on the mini-soccer field, applying mini-soccer rules. The game starts with a ball toss. While two players compete, the other four wait behind the end lines. When a goal is scored or the ball runs across one end line, two other players substitute for these first two players. In the following challenges between the same players, the one who lost the first competition will attack, from the center of the field, the opponent from a minimum distance of 3 meters. The player who finally manages to score three goals against the same opponent is the winner of the 1-on-1 Challenge and accumulates 1 point for the test. Always have one of the players who is not involved in playing the game act as referee. The official rules of mini-soccer without a goalkeeper apply.

2. 2-on-2 Challenge

A team of Players 1, 2, and 3 plays against a team of Players 4, 5, and 6; that is two teams of three players are formed. Only two of the team's members, however, may play simultaneously. Every time a goal is scored, one player of each team goes off and the third player comes in as the substitute. The team that scores more goals within 5 minutes is the winner. Every player from the winning team gets 2 points for the test.

3. Mini-Soccer 3 on 3

Players 1, 2, and 4 form one team that faces Players 3, 5, and 6 as the other team. The game is played with the official rules of mini-soccer, without a goalkeeper, during three periods of 3 minutes each. Every player of the winning team will gain 3 points for the test.

The test is won by the player with the highest number of points. If you have 12 players available, form two groups. The first three and the last three will face each other in "playoffs" for the final individual rankings of 1–6 and 7–12.

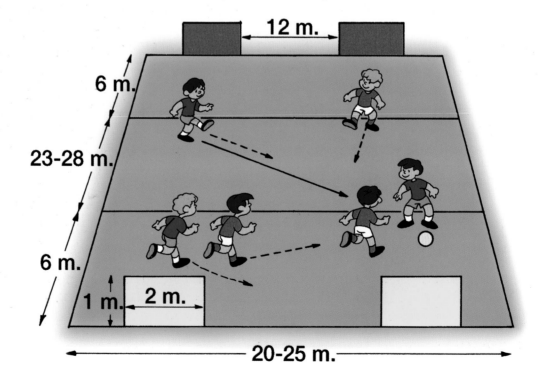

Level 2 Competitions

The variations of mini-soccer (without and later with goalkeeper), the Mini-Soccer Pentathlon, and 3-on-3 triathlon are tailor-made competitions for youngsters under 10 years of age. They all help to unlock, stimulate, and develop the innate potential of the young boys and girls, and in these competitions the coach can be more an organizer than an instructor. Because there are fewer players and a playing field of smaller dimensions, the 8- and 9-year-old players (but also older ones) will always feel capable. This sense of self-esteem is an important experience for them that can also promote soccer, perhaps instilling this game as their lifetime sport of choice.

Mini-Soccer 3 on 3 (Without Goalkeepers)

Mini-soccer without a goalkeeper is considered the ideal competition for 8-year-old soccer players. It should prepare these boys and girls to successfully play competitive mini-soccer with goalkeepers the following year. It helps prepare the children to approach the 7-on-7 game. Boys and girls may still play together on the same team.

© Jane Faircloth/Transparencies, Inc.

Tailor-made competitions in which players can demonstrate their decision-making skills will foster feelings of capability and self-esteem.

Playing Field

Mini-soccer is played in an area measuring 20 to 25 meters by 35 to 40 meters, a basketball court (14 by 26 meters), or a handball or indoor soccer field (20 by 40 meters). On each end line, there should be two 2-meters-wide goals set up with two posts, each 1 meter high. Usually the goals are set 12 meters apart (on a basketball court this can be 6 meters). The shooting zones are generally determined by straight lines, drawn parallel to the goal lines and set 5.8 meters inside the field (see the free throw line of the basketball court). On handball fields, the circles with interrupted lines in front of both goals will be used.

A goal is scored when the ball, played by an attacker from inside the opponent's shooting zone, completely crosses the goal line between the two posts of either of the two mini-goals. If the posts have been moved during the match and the ball, in the referee's opinion, completely crosses the goal line at the goal's original position, the goal still is valid.

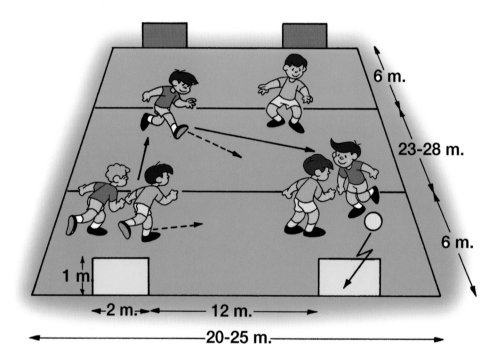

Teams

A mini-soccer team is made up of only four players, three of them being allowed to play at the same time on the field. The competition should not be played with fewer than three players per team. After either team scores a goal, one player of each team has to be substituted. These players must always enter the playing area at the centerline, after the teammate has left the field at the same spot. In case of an infringement of this rule, the other team will be awarded a free kick in front of the opponent's shooting area—but at least 3 meters away from it.

Duration

Include three 10-minute periods when only one match a day is played, with a 5-minute break between the periods. If several matches are played on the same day, the recommended duration of play is two 10-minute periods.

Technical Rules

A player may not play the ball with his hands or use violence.

➤ Free kick—For any breach of rules in any part of the field (with the exception of the defenders in their own defensive zone), a free kick is awarded for the other side. To put the ball into play, the young player may choose either to pass the ball to a teammate or to dribble it. All free kicks must be taken at a distance no less than 3 meters away from the shooting zone and with the defenders also more than 3 meters off the ball.

➤ Penalty—There is no penalty shot for an intentional breach of the rules inside of a team's own 5.8-meter zone, but the opponent will be awarded a "penalty attack," starting from the center of the field. In a penalty attack all the players, except one defender on the end line, must remain 5 meters behind the attacker in possession of the ball (see illustration). After the referee has given permission for the attack, they all may interfere in defense as well as in support. The defender starts from the end line. In case of an infringement of the rules by any defender, the free attack must be repeated.

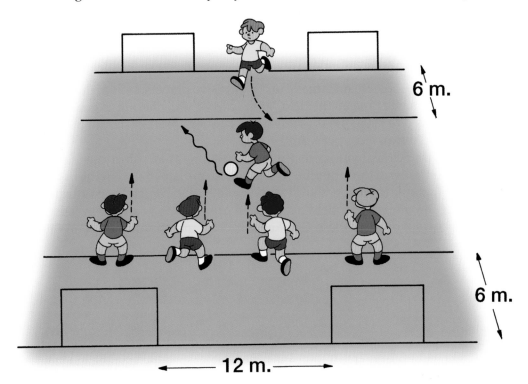

➤ Corners—There aren't any corner kicks in mini-soccer.

➤ Kick-in and side-out—The ball is brought into play with a free kick from the sideline or from the 5.8-meter line.

➤ Start and restart of the game—Always start or restart the game with a ball toss in the center of the field.

➤ Disciplinary sanctions—Temporary expulsion from play is the penalty for unsporting behavior.

Equipment

Balls—Using a No. 4 or No. 3 ball can help avoid congestion of play and also improve the youngsters' technical abilities.

Attire—All players of one team must wear the same color shirt, shorts, and socks.

Protective clothing—All players are required to wear shin guards.

Referee

A single referee supervises the match and applies the rules. To promote and train future umpires, children under 16 years of age supervise the mini-soccer matches.

Mini-Soccer 3 on 3 (With Goalkeepers)

Mini-soccer with a goalkeeper is considered the ideal team competition for the 9-year-old players. It allows them to spend an entire season preparing for the greater demands of the 7-on-7 game, which they will play the following year.

Playing Field

This game uses the same field dimensions as in mini-soccer without a goalkeeper.

Teams

A mini-soccer team is made up by only five players, four of them being allowed to play at the same time on the field, with one of them playing as goalkeeper. The goalie isn't allowed to leave the shooting area. The competition should not be played with fewer than four players per team.

After either team scores a goal, both teams must substitute one player! These players must enter at the centerline, after their teammates have left the field from the same spot. If this rule is broken, the other side will be awarded a "penalty attack" from the center of the mini-soccer field against the opponent's goalkeeper. See the rules for "Mini-Soccer 3 on 3 (Without Goalkeepers)" for more information on the penalty attack.

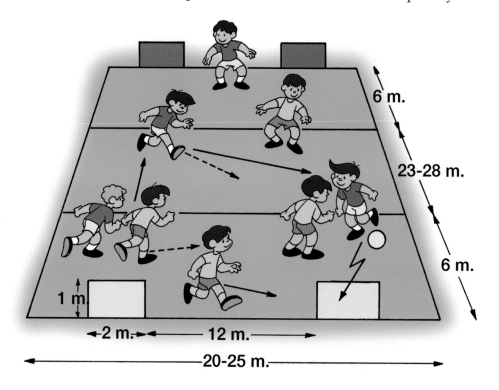

Duration

If only one match takes place for the 9-year-old players, the competition should last for three 10-minute periods, with 5-minute breaks between the periods. If several matches are played on the same day (for instance, in a tournament or festival), the recommended duration of play is two 10-minute periods.

Technical Rules

A player may not play the ball with the hand or use violence.

➤ Free Kick—For any breach of rules in any part of the field (except for the defenders in their own defensive zone), a free kick is awarded for the other side. To put the ball into play, the player may choose either to pass the ball to a teammate or to dribble it. All free kicks must be taken at a distance of no less than 3 meters away from the shooting zone, with the defenders also more than 3 meters off the ball.

➤ Penalty—There is no penalty shot for an intentional breach of the rules inside a team's own 5.8-meter zone, but the opponent will be awarded a "penalty attack," which starts from the center of the field. In a penalty attack all the players, except the goalkeepers, must remain 5 meters behind the attacker in possession of the ball. After the referee has given permission for the attack, they all may interfere in defense as well as in support. The goalkeeper starts his defense from the end line. In case of an infringement of the rules by any defender, the free attack is repeated.

➤ Corners—Mini-soccer with goalkeepers has no corner kicks.

➤ Kick-ins and side-outs—The ball is brought into play with a free kick from the sideline or from the 5.8-meter line.

➤ Start and restart of the game—Always start or restart the game with a ball toss in the center of the field.

Equipment

The equipment needs (balls, shin guards, and attire) and the referee recommendations are the same as given in the rules of mini-soccer without goalkeepers.

Mini-Soccer 3-on-3 Variations

To add even more variety to the training program, let players experiment with and enjoy these eight mini-soccer variations.

1. Make it, Take it—The team that scores with a dribble through one of the 6-meter-wide goals continues attacking but must now play to the opposite two goals. Immediately after the score, no tackle is allowed in the shooting zone.

2. Choose Any Goal—A goal can be scored by dribbling the ball through any of the four 6-meter-wide goals.

3. Attack Diagonally Opposite Goals—Each team defends two diagonally opposite goals and scores through the two remaining ones with a dribble or a shot from inside the shooting zone.

4. Three Teams—One team in the center of the field attacks in both directions. It alternately approaches the two 6-meter-wide goals of the other two teams. These defend, with two players in front of the shooting zone and a third one always inside the zone to be able to cover them in case of necessity.

5. Through Passing—A goal can be scored only with a pass from outside the shooting zone through the less-defended goal of the opponents. None of the players may enter the two 5.8-meter shooting zones. It's smart to use reserve balls; although accuracy is the objective, that doesn't always occur.

6. Additional Shooting—The mini-soccer field is drawn between the offside line and the centerline of the 7-on-7 soccer field. After one team manages to dribble the ball across one of the two opposing 6-meter-wide goals on the offside line or centerline, *within 2 seconds* the same attacker must execute a shot toward a 7-on-7–sized goal. The shot must be from a distance of 11 meters, and a neutral goalkeeper should be defending.

7. Three Times "1 on 1"—One player of each team faces the other in a 1-on-1 situation. All pairs play at the same time, with the objective being to dribble the ball across one of the opponent's 6-meter-wide goals. Whoever scores more often in 2 minutes wins. After a goal is scored, the game is restarted from the center of the field by the opponent, with the other player at a distance of at least 3 meters. It's also possible to determine the winning team by adding up the goals scored by the three team members.

8. Channeling—This is a variation to develop an aspect of mini-soccer. To encourage the defenders to practice the channeling of the opponent toward an agreed zone of the field, a different number of points is awarded for scoring in the left goal (for instance, only 1 point) or the right goal (for instance, 3 points).

Mini-Soccer Pentathlon

There is no doubt that a young player's versatile preparation is a prerequisite for successfully developing more complex skills later. *The learning of soccer-specific skills becomes extremely difficult if fundamental skills and coordination have been poorly developed.*

As most youth coaches have an enormous desire to win the next match (they hope to become better recognized by the parents and their club), they generally focus the teaching and learning processes exclusively on those soccer-specific skills that, to a high extent, determine the competition's result. They train what the competition obviously demands. Because a competition demands that players execute and apply basic soccer skills, the coaches concentrate exclusively on the players' acquiring and consolidating these skills. There is no time left for creating a rich and varied activity program that forms a solid base for future successes, fewer injuries, fewer dropouts, and greater motivation in soccer.

To encourage (or even oblige) youth soccer coaches to include multilateral activities in the training they offer, it's essential to change how we structure official competitions for beginners. When the actual competition demands only soccer knowledge and specific skills, it's logical that coaches concentrate the players' efforts on practicing them again and again. However, when this competition is replaced by a multilateral one that demands many other abilities—capacities essential for a complete soccer player—it becomes an entirely different matter.

A Mini-Soccer Pentathlon springs from these ideas and convictions. To help players win the pentathlon, their coaches will prepare the young players not only with specific skills for the three mini-soccer matches but also with a multilateral training program for the two other games, which may change every month, inserted between the mini-soccer games.

Taking Mini-Soccer Further Toward 7-on-7 Soccer

Progression of Mini-Soccer Competitions

1.   3-on-3 Mini-Soccer Without Goalkeeper*—One player on each side must remain in his or her own shooting area.

2.   3-on-3 Mini-Soccer Without Goalkeeper—One player on each side must remain in the opposing shooting area.

3.   3-on-3 Mini-Soccer Without Goalkeeper**—A goal may be scored only by dribbling the ball across one of the two wider goal areas.

4.   3-on-3 Mini-Soccer Without Goalkeeper**—A goal may be scored only from inside the opposing shooting area.

5.   3-on-3 Mini-Soccer Without Goalkeeper—A goal may be scored only from some point in the center of the field.

6.   3-on-3 Mini-Soccer With Goalkeeper***—A goal may be scored only from inside the opposing shooting area.

7.   3-on-3 Mini-Soccer With Goalkeeper—A goal may be scored only from some point of the center of the field.

8.   3 on 3 on the Mini-Soccer Field With Two Front Runners—Positioned inside the two opposite goals on the end line, two front runners wait for through passes out of the midfield played by their three teammates.

9.   3 on 3 on the Mini-Soccer Field With Two Front Runners and an Additional Defender (6 on 6)—The front runners are positioned in the opposing goal area, and an opposing defender is there to intercept the through passes made to them.

10.   3 on 3 on the Mini-Soccer Field With Two Front Runners, a Defender, and a Goalkeeper (7 on 7)—Three midfield players pass the ball out of the midfield to one of their two front runners. The front runners are both waiting in the opponent's goal area, always considering the play of a fourth defender, positioned in front of them. If this defender can't intercept the pass inside his area, he recovers and prevents the two attackers from further developing the attack (this, then, becomes a 2-on-1 situation, with scoring against a goalkeeper who defends a regular 7-on-7 size goal, established 15 meters behind the two goal cone goals.

11.   7-on-7 Soccer****—Play a free game, without limiting what the players can do, that is, their positions and functions (as in the previous games).

*The first three games form part of the Mini-Soccer Pentathlon.
**See the official rules of Mini-Soccer Without Goalkeepers.
***See the official rules of Mini-Soccer With Goalkeepers.
****See the official rules of 7-on-7 Soccer.

1. Mini-Soccer 3 on 3 (Variation 1)

One player of each team must remain within the team's proper shooting zone until one or the other team manages to score a goal. After a goal is scored, all players of both teams must rotate. With the exception of this rule and having no substitutes, the official rules of mini-soccer are in force.

Duration of the game: two periods of 7.5 minutes.

2. Coordination Relay

Each team lines up in one of the two goals of one shooting area. Give a visual signal for the first player of each team to do the following:

- Run 6 meters to the limit of the shooting area in order to touch the line with one of his feet (1).

- Return to the starting line, where she knocks down one of the two cones of his goal (2), using the other foot.
- Turn to the cone situated in the center of the mini-soccer field (3), run around it, and head toward the two balls (which lie forming a 1.5-meter-wide "river").
- Jump over the "river" (4).
- Continue to run toward the starting line to knock down the second cone of the goal (5) with one foot.

Once the cone has been knocked down, the next player starts doing the same routine. Instead of knocking down the cones, his function, however, now is to put them in a correct position again, using his hands. Each player must run twice.

The team wins that manages to first complete two relays.

3. Mini-Soccer 3 on 3 (Variation II)

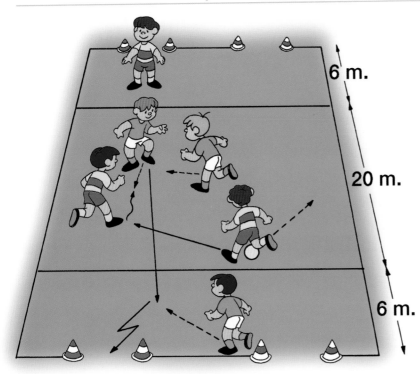

6 m.

20 m.

6 m.

One player of each team must remain in the opposing shooting zone where he stays open to receive through passes and then score in either goal. After every goal, the three players from each team must rotate positions. Once the ball enters one of the shooting areas, all four midfield players may move into these zones for defending or for giving support.

Duration of the game: two periods of 7.5 minutes.

4. Tag Two Robbers

One team, made up of three "police officers," is stationed in its headquarters (one of the two goals of one shooting zone). The coach signals the start of play, and they run one after another into the shooting zone where three robbers have to avoid being tagged by a police officer (cop). Once a cop has managed to touch two different opponents, he returns quickly to his headquarters to give his fellow cop (by tagging her with a touch) the right to chase two of the three escaping robbers. The relay or tag is over when all three police officers have done their job and have returned to the starting point. If one of the three escaping players moves out of the shooting zone, this counts as a successful tag by the cop. To establish the winner, keep track of the time each team needs to "arrest" the thieves with two touches. Each team must tag and escape twice.

5. Mini-Soccer 3 on 3 (Variation III)

The official rules of "Mini-Soccer 3 on 3 Without Goalkeepers" (and without substitutes) apply. Duration of the game: two periods of 7.5 minutes.

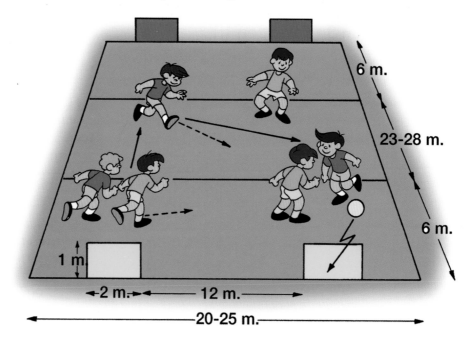

The duration of the entire pentathlon is about 70 minutes. The team that wins at least three of the five tests is declared grand winner of the Mini-Soccer Pentathlon.

3-on-3 Triathlon

Just like the 2-on-2 triathlon in Level 1, the 3-on-3 triathlon should be included periodically as part of the training program. The triathlon helps players learn to read situations and react to the moves of two other teammates as well as to a maximum of three defenders.

The following figure illustrates the ideal organization for the triathlon competition. In this example, the "Asian" teams compete against the "American" teams until a winner is decided. The blank spaces next to each game are for coaches to use in recording scores.

Asia against America

Teams	Korea	Oman	Japan	Malaysia
Names of players				

Teams	Argentina	Chile	USA	Uruguay
Names of players				

First game: 3-on-3 with four intersecting goals (4 × 3 min.)

Scores

KOR-ARG		
OMA-CHI		
JPN-USA		
MAL-URU		

Second game: 3-on-2 with counterattack (4 × 3 min.)

Scores

KOR-CHI		
OMA-USA		
JPN-URU		
MAL-ARG		

Third game: 3-on-3 with two wide goals (4 × 3 min.)

Scores

MAL-CHI		
JPN-ARG		
OMA-URU		
KOR-USA		

Final result: Asia against America _____ _____
(sum of victories)

Technical delegate: _____

Note: During the triathlon, changing the composition of the team is not permitted.

Organization of the 3-on-3 triathlon.

1. 3 on 3 With Four Goals

- Each team attacks the two wide goals assigned to them and defends the other two.
- Throw the ball to start the game.
- There are no throw-ins.
- Free kicks or dribbles should be taken not less than 3 meters from the goal lines.
- To score, a player has to dribble the ball from a spot inside the field across one of the two opposing goal areas.
- Duration of the game: four periods of 3 minutes each, with 1 minute's rest between them.

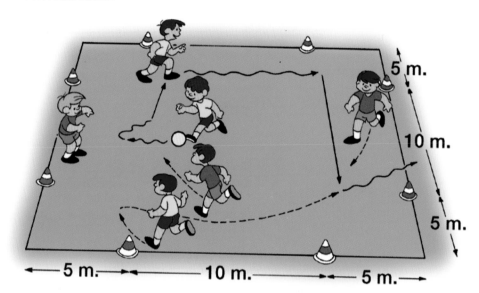

2. 3 on 2 With Counterattack

- Play four periods of 3 minutes.
- During the 3 minutes, one team alternately attacks the two 20-meter-wide goals.
- Two opponents defend the goal, while the third is placed in the opposite goal area waiting for a pass from his teammates.
- After each attack, the defenders have to rotate: one of the two joins his or her teammate in the opposite goal so that the situation always is 3 on 2.
- Once the ball has been lost by the attackers, these players should tackle back immediately—but never from behind the centerline.
- A goal is scored with a dribble across the goal line.
- Both teams may score.
- Change positions after every 3 minutes, switching between the attackers and defenders.
- Free kicks or dribbles should be from no less than 3 meters from the goal line.

20 m.

3. 3 on 3 With Two Wide Goals

- Set the dimensions of the playing area as in the illustration (20 by 20 meters, with goals 20-meters wide).
- Use a ball toss to start the game.
- Free kicks and dribbles should be from no less than 3 meters from the goal line.
- To score, the ball must be dribbled across the opposing goal line.
- Duration of the game: four periods of 3 minutes.

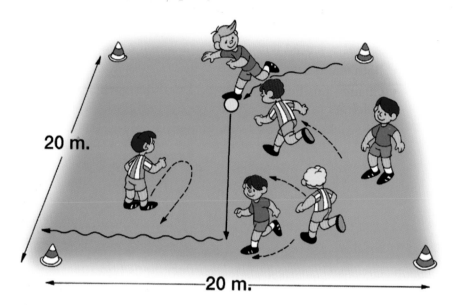

All activities proposed in Levels 1 and 2 have as the objective that players under 10 years of age can learn to enjoy and successfully play mini-soccer. All the games (of basic abilities, as well as the simplified games) presented in this chapter together with their tailor-made competitions, are seen as so many pieces forming a complete puzzle, one called mini-soccer. As the youngsters play mini-soccer, your reviewing with them the games for basic abilities in Level 1 and the more difficult and complex ones of Level 2 (all of these should be considered as corrective exercises for mini-soccer) will help them improve and consolidate most of the soccer fundamentals. In addition, having the players practice the different variations of mini-soccer (including the Mini-Soccer Pentathlon), thanks to the two goals to attack and to defend, further consolidates these basic skills. And players gain new experience in such important capacities as perception, anticipation, and decision making, essential for the preparation of the 7-on-7 soccer game.

PART III

Coaching Players 10 Years and Up

The third level of the Soccer Development Model further develops players' technical and tactical abilities and capacities through a variety of simplified games for teams of three players and later for teams of four players. In addition, Level 3 presents a specialized training program for developing young goalkeepers. Before putting these programs to work, however, coaches should understand a little more about their players.

People who teach players between 10 and 12 years old have a rewarding field of operation. As many sources confirm, at this later stage of their childhood, youngsters are in a "golden age of motor learning" (Diem lectures). A sum of favorable conditions exist in the biological, psychological, and motor spheres. Body and mind are in harmony and balance. Leaving the dream world behind, children now strive, more than ever before, for realism. The world of the unreal, incomprehensible, or fantasy is declined. Their capacity for abstraction (that is, separating the essential from the less important) develops, and this advance favors their understanding and reading of game situations. For the first time, the sense awakens that all action is submitted to certain general rules.

Prepubescent soccer players still have an urge for physical activity, which favors their intrinsic motivation to get more and more involved in sports. However, instead of looking to meet their insatiable or unlicensed need for movement, as happened in the years before 10, the youth now strive after good performance, profiting from the fact that their movements are now more controlled and carried out more economically and with single-mindeness. Trying to emulate the sport model, youngsters can show a real dedication for continuous improvement. In fact, children of 10 to 12 years of age are even more motivated to practice hard when a game is organized in which they can *demonstrate their abilities* to their friends and to the opposing team.

What does this mean for coaches? At this stage of the young soccer players' evolution, their teachers must make a transition from simply presenting a great variety of multilateral and specific soccer activities to preparing a more systematic, intensive, and purposeful practice of technical-tactical aspects of the soccer game.

Exercises for developing speed, coordination, and aerobic resistance are to be considered the pillars of multilateral development, while the understanding, practice, and mastering of a great variety of simplified soccer games (played with teams of three or four players) are the cornerstones of building their specific improvement.

5

Games for 7-on-7 Soccer

Level 3

In soccer the brain counts a lot. All players have two legs, two hands, two ears, and two eyes, but only one brain.

Understanding soccer involves comprehending how the game develops and works. The coach must teach players not only many individual and team skills but also thinking skills. Without understanding the most common situations that occur in the game, it's difficult to make correct decisions; without mastering the playing skills, on the other hand, these decisions cannot be carried out. The most natural way to develop "reading and reacting skills" is to expose the youngsters to many different simplified games, which teach the players how to be in the right place on the field at the right time. This is precisely what the simplified games in Level 3 are meant to do.

Reading the game means observing and analyzing the location of teammates, opponents, and the ball as well as the speed and direction of play. This ability allows participants to anticipate the next play.

The Basic Three Game Situations

Everything that happens on the soccer field occurs in one of these three situations:

1. The ball is loose and neither team has it.
2. The team has the ball on offense.
3. The team is on defense, preventing the opponent from scoring.

These three conditions frequently change phases, but during each of them the player must constantly read and react. How to react depends on the player's position in relation to the ball and his or her proximity to the team's own goal. A golden rule, a precondition of interpreting any game situation, is that the player must face the play to see the situation; only then can he react. Turning one's back to the play (as many front runners do, for example, when they receive the ball) is a cardinal mistake.

Loose-Ball Game

The reaction of the player closest to the loose ball dictates whether the team will be on offense or defense. This player's first thought should be defensive until he or she can read the situation perfectly. Generally, the closest player's reaction to a loose ball is to become the ball carrier. While the faceoff is going on, all other players involved in the game situation (teammates of the possible attacker and those of the possible defender) must know their roles in advance in case their teammate wins, loses, or draws in the loose-ball game. During the loose-ball game, does the player correctly recognize his proximity or closeness to the ball? Does he know how to assess his distance to it (in relation to that of the nearest opponent), taking into account his and the opponent's speeds? When the situation is not clear, does he recognize whether his distance to his own goal allows him to make an offensive or a defensive decision? *Statistics have shown that the team that wins the most loose balls usually also wins the game.* Therefore, to improve a win-lose record, the players should concentrate on winning those loose balls!

Offensive Game

While the player who is closest to the ball chooses between beating his opponent or passing the ball, he also considers his teammates' positions farther away from the ball. Some of them should support the ball carrier and join the attack. The more support the ball carrier receives, the more options he has. He should have at least three safe passes

The team that captures the most loose balls is also likely to win the game.

to his fellow players, who by their running free give width and depth to the attack and help spread the defense. The width of the attack is determined by how far apart the players position themselves in the outside lanes and by their occupying all attacking positions. It also depends on where they are in the center lane, from which distribution or passing of the ball is the easiest. The depth of the attack is the distance between the players who are closest to and farthest from the ball. Whenever possible, there should be low, medium, and high depths on the attack.

Knowing when not to move is as important as knowing what move to make.

How quickly the transition takes place from defense to offense or vice versa is of great importance. Modern soccer is a game of quick transitions. The most dangerous attacking situations can be created after a successful tackle, when the new attack is launched literally within a second. Generally it takes more time for the defense to recognize that they have to change their roles.

Attackers who make use of quick transitions from defense to offense generally attack an unorganized defense, whereas a slow transition might result in an attack being against an already-organized defense.

The first player, who either beats his opponent and carries the ball up the field (or passes it to the closest supporting player), and the nearest supporting player are the key players. When an attacker without the ball creates passing options, the transition becomes much quicker than in the case when the ball carrier is forced to keep running with the ball in order to create space and time for himself.

Defensive Game

The player of the other team who was not as close to the ball in the loose-ball situation then becomes the defender. He is the key player on defense: after all, his quickness and kinds of movements determine how his teammates have to defend. If he is aggressive, his teammates defend by close 1-on-1 coverage, but if the first opponent is passive, his teammates only cover the zone.

He should quickly put pressure on the ball carrier, at the same time receiving immediate support from the closest teammate and the rest of the defending players. The role of these defenders depends on their distance from the ball also and whether they are the second-, third-, fourth-, or fifth-closest player to the checking defender. While facing the ball and personal opponent simultaneously, with the head swiveling or turning at all times, the defender may decide to switch opponents without forgetting to choose a correct position between the attacker and his own goal. Does the closest checking player take the space away from the ball carrier? Does she get immediate support by teammate defenders? Does the whole defensive unit still give immediate support to the checking player after it seems obvious that the opponent will win the loose ball? The ball carrier who is being checked by the closest defender often is not the most dangerous player—someone among the potential pass receivers is.

It is part of a coach's functions to watch how her defenders perform in these four types of play or roles:

1. An opponent with the ball
2. A player checking the ball carrier
3. Opponents who are supporting the ball carrier
4. Players who are covering the checking defender or the area away from the ball

The more a young soccer player understands the game, the better he or she will be able to see, read, and react to all game situations.

Organizing the Training Session

Here are a few recommendations for structuring a training session for players aged 10 to 12 years old:

1. Instead of starting with a warm-up (which is not mandatory for children younger than 12 years), the session should always begin with a simplified game in which the coach presents specific game-related problems to the few players of each team.

2. During a 10-minute game, observe and analyze the technical and tactical playing performance of the players. After the game, assign and have carried out a series of corrective exercises to ameliorate the problem situations you have discovered. The choice of these corrective exercises depends on the technical-tactical aspects that have lowered the quality of play (for example, you might work on tackling at the right instant, not too late and not too early, or on receiving skills).

3. After isolated skill practice (always seen as a function of performance in the simplified game), the game resumes. See whether the weaknesses you had previously noticed have been overcome with the help of the corrective exercises or whether other aspects of the game still need improvement. Through systematic questioning from you

as coach, players can become aware of the importance of specific soccer knowledge; ask them to work out the correct patterns.

Other training tips:

➤ To facilitate the observation, analysis, decision making, and motor response of the young players, no more than seven youngsters per team should participate in the simplified game.

➤ The space in which the simplified game takes place should initially be rather wide and deep to give the players enough time to decide their moves and enough space to carry them out. Only when the level of technique is high enough to allow the players to draw their attention to other aspects inherent in the soccer game, should the coach reduce the time and space. Gradually, then, both these parameters become similar to those of the official competition.

➤ Learning and perfecting basic abilities and capacities must be considered an important part of each training session. *The more game-like the situation is that you present to the players in training, the more they are able to transfer the experience to the game.*

➤ Alternate exercises and games of high intensity with those of low intensity.

➤ As the capacity of play improves, the multilateral games are introduced less often in the training sessions. The multilateral games, apart from being used to contribute to the intensity, variety, and the fun of the training, ensure the important and indispensable development of basic abilities and capacities.

➤ The training of coordination skills and physical capacities (such as various kinds of resistance, speed, and strength) should be an integral part of the practice session.

➤ At this stage, Level 3, thanks to players' improved perception and capacity of abstraction, instead of explaining a determined skill or tactical move in detail, coaches need provide only a demonstration of the sequence. This is usually sufficient to allow them to reproduce the same pattern with ease.

➤ It is especially important for coaches to treat everyone the same way and not show favoritism. Generally, prepubescent soccer players are pleased with their coaches if they are fair with everyone.

Simplified Games for 3 on 3

The simplified game is still an ideal framework for discovering, understanding, and resolving specific game-related problems.

1st   Simplified Game
Maintaining Ball Possession 3 on 1

Mark off two adjacent squares of 8 to 10 meters. In one, three attackers keep the ball against one defender. In the other square, two of the defender's teammates wait for a pass from their colleague if his or her defense succeeds. Once they control the ball, the former defender joins the two teammates to try to keep possession of the ball in another 3-on-1 situation.

A switch of play from one to the other playing area also occurs when one of the attackers infringes on the rules or the ball played by the attackers runs out of the limited zone. In both cases the defender kicks the ball from the sideline to one teammate in the adjacent area, with the opponents staying at a distance of at least 3 meters. Immediately after the successful kick-in, the player joins his or her team members in the adjacent area. Here it's their turn to keep possession in the new 3-on-1 situation. If one defender runs out of energy, he or she may switch positions with a teammate of the adjacent square. After a 5-minute practice, organize a competition with one player of the adjacent area counting the seconds of ball possession.

Duration of the game: three periods of 3 minutes each. After 9 minutes of play the team that achieves the best time is winner. After every change of area (squares), a rotation takes place in the defending team.

VARIATIONS

➤ After passing to a teammate, the attacker must move at least 5 meters out of his former position. Using this rule helps develop the players' orientation and perception.

➤ To stimulate ball control, the attackers must play aerial passes. Passes along the ground are not allowed.

➤ Count (keep track of) the number of successive passes played exclusively with the less-skilled foot.

➤ Count the number of first-time passes during one ball possession.

➤ Have three attackers face one defender in both playing areas. The group that keeps the ball longer wins.

TRAINING OBJECTIVES

- Learn to avoid playing the ball into the opponent's range of action.
- Learn to pass the ball with precise timing, not too early and not too late.
- Learn when to pass and when to dribble.
- Learn to pass the ball accurately, fast enough, and without indicating its trajectory.

- After passing the ball, be prepared to receive it again; learn to support the ball carrier and consider the support given by the teammates.
- As defender, learn to press the ball carrier and anticipate the opponent's play.

CORRECTIVE EXERCISES

Most of the "Games for Passing, Receiving, and Shooting," as well as all the 2-on-2 simplified games make good material for remedial work.

2nd Simplified Game
Fast Attack

Set up a 7-on-7 soccer field. Divide the youngsters into three attackers and three defenders, with an additional goalkeeper. The three attackers start with the ball from the centerline of the field and try to beat a defender (the "sweeper") situated in front of the penalty zone. The attackers may only score goals from inside the zone. When the attackers first touch the ball on the centerline, the two defenders situated 8 to 12 meters behind them begin pursuit, trying to help the sweeper, who is doing everything possible to delay the attack.

The attack ends

- when a goal is scored,
- when the attackers commit a rules' infringement,
- when the ball is played out of the playing area, or
- when the defenders can touch the ball three consecutive times or pass it once between them.

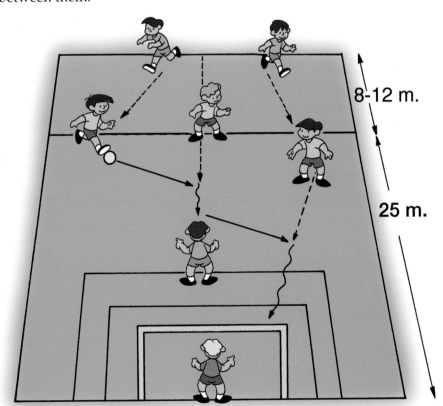

When the defenders commit an infringement of the rules inside the penalty area, a penalty kick from 9 meters against a neutral goalkeeper is awarded. After five fast attacks, both teams switch positions and functions until each team has defended and attacked 10 times. After each attack the "sweeper" rotates. In the second series of attacks, the players in attack as well as in defense must assume different playing positions. The defenders who support the sweeper now should also start from different positions on both sidelines.

After the competition, use probing, open questions to work out with your players what the most effective fast attack would be, considering aspects of the dribble, of passing, of controlling the ball, and of shooting.

VARIATIONS

➤ After a successful tackle or interception, the defenders must pass the ball across the centerline or through one of the two goals, which should be established on the centerline in the wing positions.

➤ The attackers may not pass the ball more than three times (or you can specify twice).

➤ Three attackers play against two defenders, with one tackling from behind. (This variation is for more advanced players.)

TRAINING OBJECTIVES

- Consolidate the execution of the basic skills of dribbling, passing, receiving, and scoring at high speed.
- Create correct habits for counterattacking: for instance, initially pass the ball from the depth of the field directly into the path of the teammate, receive the ball on the run, use direct passes instead of receiving and controlling the ball before making a pass.
- Learn to read the game: know when to pass or not pass the ball, always considering the actions of the three defenders that condition the attacking play.
- Learn to look out for an effective attack. Three offensive actions are better than four. After carrying the ball to the third defender, a diagonal pass into the run of one of the supporting players to either side who then shoots from a safe distance is likely to assure a successful conclusion of the fast attack.
- Learn to cooperate in defense and to systematically delay the counterattack.

CORRECTIVE EXERCISES

The following corrective exercises should be included in the training program as needed.

1. Dribble and Tag Games

Review the "Dribbling Games" and especially the tag games in chapter 3, "Games for Basic Abilities and Capacities."

2. Tackling From Behind

One attacker starts with a ball from the centerline of a mini-soccer field. A defender stands 1 meter behind this attacker and follows him or her, trying to execute a successful tackle before the attacker can control the ball in the penalty area.

For attacking with success the forward must

- move quickly,
- invade the path of the defender who nears him or her (to avoid a collision and an infringement of the rules, the defender must slow down his running speed), or
- feint a stop of the ball; while the defender reacts to this new situation and prepares a tackle, the attacker can suddenly change speed and escape.

After three attacks, the defender and attacker switch functions. Make sure that both players have a similar capacity in running speed.

3. Delaying the Opponents' Attack

Review the rules of a "penalty attack" in the mini-soccer competition (chapter 4). This practice uses six players. After the coach's visual signal, an attacker in the center of the mini-soccer field dribbles the ball toward one of the two opposing goals defended by an opponent who starts from the end line. This defender closes down on the attacker and channels him to one side of the field. Meanwhile, after the iniation of the attack, four other players (two attackers and two defenders) run from the opposite end line onto the field to support the single attacker or to tackle or intercept his pass.

A goal can be scored only from inside the shooting zone. The attack of the three (one plus two) finishes, when

- one of the attackers scores,
- the attackers lose the ball to the defenders,
- an attacker infringes on the rules, or
- when the ball runs out of play.

The players rotate positions on the second and third attacks, and the teams switch functions after each full rotation. The team which manages to score the highest number of goals in six attacks wins. In case of a foul by one of the defenders, the attack has to be repeated.

As a variation, the two supporting defenders and the two supporting attackers may start from the line of the shooting zone, thus putting more pressure on the attackers.

3rd **Simplified Game**

3 on 1 Plus a Defender Who Covers

15-20 m.

15 m.

The game, which involves six players, is played between the centerline and one line of the penalty area of a 7-on-7 soccer field. Set up cones to establish two 15-meter-wide goal areas on the penalty-area lines (see illustration). Three players are in possession of the ball and start their attack from the centerline, aiming to alternately control the ball in the goal area on the penalty-area line. This goal, as well as the one established on the centerline, is defended by a single defender who must always remain on the same line without entering the field. One additional midfield player must always tackle first. After the conclusion of the first attack, with or without success, the three attackers turn around to attack the opposite wide goal, again tackled by the same midfield player and a third defender who covers him while always remaining on the goal line.

An attack finishes

- when a goal is scored with a dribble across one of the two goals,
- when the ball runs out of play, or
- when one of the two defenders wins the ball and manages to execute a pass to one of his two teammates.

Duration of the match: three periods of 2 minutes until every defender has played once in each position. The forwards are also asked to switch their positions every 2 minutes.

VARIATIONS

➤ When the midfield player wins the ball, the other two defenders may leave their positions on the end lines and move to receive a pass. If they manage to pass the ball twice, they now attack, while the former three attackers have to take over the defending positions and functions.

➤ After dribbling the ball across the goal line, the attackers have to score from a distance of 11 meters into a goal defended by a neutral goalkeeper.

TRAINING OBJECTIVES

See the First Simplified Game for 3 on 3, which has the same objectives.

CORRECTIVE EXERCISES

Choose from earlier simplified games for keeping possession of the ball in 2-on-1 or 3-on-1 situations.

Simplified Game

3 on 3 With Four Intersecting Goals

Teams of three players simultaneously defend two opposite goal areas (which should be 10 meters wide) and attack the other two. The illustration shows the setup and field dimensions.

The game is started by a ball toss into the center of the square. When the ball runs across any sideline, there is a kick-in from where the ball left the playing area. During a free kick or kick-in, the opponents must be at least 3 meters away from the ball. To score, a player has to dribble the ball through one of two opposing goals.

Duration of the game: four periods of 3 minutes.

VARIATIONS

➤ Use the same variations as for the game "2 on 2 With Four Intersecting Goals."

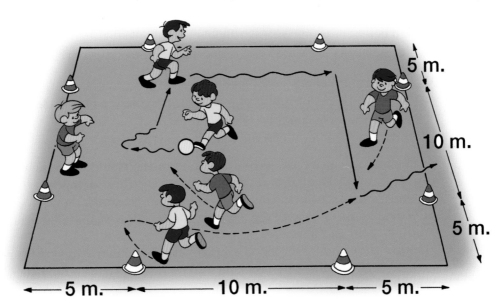

TRAINING OBJECTIVES

- Practice and consolidate the technical and tactical objectives of the game "2 on 2 With Four Intersecting Goals" and of the previous simplified games.
- Learn to always attack the goal that is less defended.
- Learn to always attack in a triangular formation, while the defense must assure width and depth (cover), and be able to pressure the ball carrier to force him to commit mistakes.
- Ensure width and depth coverage.
- In attack, learn to watch for a 2-on-1 situation—and to avoid the 1-on-1 situation.
- Be able to suddenly change the direction and rhythm of the attack without dribbling the ball too close to a defender.
- In defense, learn to pressure the ball carrier to force him to commit mistakes.
- Learn to delay the tackle to gain time for receiving the support of a teammate.
- Defending 1 on 2, learn to delay the tackle to avoid getting outplayed before the support of a teammate arrives.
- Learn to channel the opponent's play into the desired direction (for instance, into a teammate's tackling area or away from the goal).

CORRECTIVE EXERCISES

See the simplified game "2 on 2 With Four Goals."

5th Simplified Game
3 on 2 With Counterattack

Use a 7-on-7 soccer field with two 20-meter-wide goals established on the centerline and one penalty-area line. One team of three players alternately attacks the two goals. Two of the three opponents always defend the goal that is being attacked to prevent the attackers from dribbling the ball across their goal line. Meanwhile their third opponent remains in the opposite goal, ready to receive a pass from one of his team's two other defenders, should they manage to win the ball from the attackers. After receiving the ball, the third defender scores with a dribble across his own goal line without any tackle back from the attackers (they may tackle only in the upper part of the field). An attack ends

- when the attackers score a goal,
- when the ball runs out of the playing area (across one of the end lines), or
- when the defense, after having recovered the ball and passed it across the imaginary centerline to the third defender, scores.

After the conclusion of each attack, one of the two defenders must quickly run toward the opposite goal to reestablish (with the third defender) the 3 attackers on 2 defenders. In case of an infringement of the rules by an attacker, a free kick is awarded to the defenders—still with the attackers being allowed to defend only in the upper part of the field and never beyond the centerline.

During a free kick for the attackers (taken no closer than 3 meters from the goal line), the defenders, too, must remain at least 3 meters away from the ball.

Duration of the game: 10 attacks for each team or, for more advanced players, four periods of 3 minutes each.

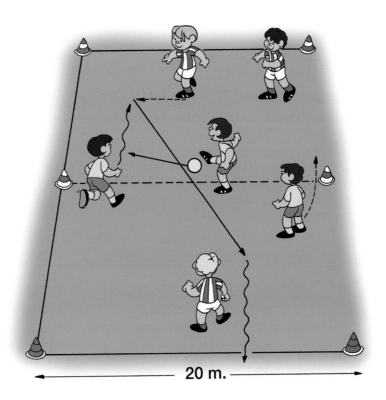

20 m.

VARIATIONS

➤ The three defenders don't have to switch positions. Therefore, the attackers practice the 3-on-1 attack at one goal line, and the 3-on-2 attack at the other goal.

➤ Instead of using two 20-meter-wide goals, the game is played using four 6-meter-wide goals (as a type of mini-soccer).

➤ Behind each end line a soccer goal is established at a distance of 11 meters. Immediately after a control on this end line, the same attacker practices shooting with a neutral goalkeeper.

TRAINING OBJECTIVES

- Practice and consolidate the technical and tactical objectives of the "2 on 1 With Counterattack" and the previous simplified games 3 on 3.
- Learn to systematically create the 2-on-1 situation in attack and to achieve a high percentage of success.
- Learn to tackle back immediately after losing possession of the ball.
- As defenders, acquire the patience to wait for the best moment for tackling or intercepting the ball.
- As defenders, learn to force the attacker to play the ball in the desired direction.
- As defenders, learn to counterattack quickly.
- As defenders, think continuously about what to do next, not forgetting to switch positions after an attack is concluded.

CORRECTIVE EXERCISES

Use the first four of the 2-on-2 simplified games.

Simplified Game

Three Teams on Two Wide Goals

Use a 7-on-7 soccer field between the two offside lines. One team of three players is in the center of the field and alternately attacks one of the two wide goals established on the offside lines. This goal and the opposite one are each defended by (a) two opponents (from the two other teams) who play midfield, well in front of the offside line, and (b) a third one who covers them without being allowed to tackle, being away from the line.

The attackers have 10 attacks (5 toward each goal) in which to try to dribble the ball as often as possible across this line (to get 1 point) and score in a goal area (6 meters by 2 meters) without (or later with) a goalkeeper (to get 2 points). After every three attacks, the cover defender changes with one of the other defenders on his team who is in front of him. An attack finishes

- when a goal is scored,
- when the ball runs across one offside line or a goal line,
- when a defender gets possession of the ball and passes it to a teammate, or
- when the attackers commit an infringement of the rules.

The winning team is the one that gets most points in 10 attacks.

30-40 m.

VARIATIONS

➤ Each 3-on-3 team has 2 minutes to score a maximum number of goals. The faster they develop their attacks, the more chances exist to score.

➤ The teams change, depending on the outcome of the attack. When the defenders manage to win the ball and also execute at least two passes on their team, they become attackers of the opposite goal. While launching their attack, the former attackers defend the goal where their attack failed. If the attackers score with a dribble, they continue to attack.

➤ The attackers can only play a maximum of 4 (or 3) passes, and work to find the most effective attack.

➤ To simplify the attack and practice goal scoring, the defense either has one defender in front of the offside line, one defender who covers playing on the offside line, and a goalkeeper; two defenders playing on the offside line only and a goalkeeper; or two defenders in front of the offside line and a goalkeeper.

TRAINING OBJECTIVES

- The attackers learn that before passing the ball, they should consider not only the positions and actions of the defenders but also the movement of the covering defender on the offside line.
- Understand how essential it is that the attacker in the center is the one who has possession of the ball—either when the defenders are close or when one defender is going to execute a tackle.
- Consolidate the skills learned in the previous simplified games, and especially the principles of assuring width and depth in attack.

CORRECTIVE EXERCISES

Use the first five of the simplified games for 2 on 2.

7th Simplified Game
Maintaining Ball Possession 3 on 2

12-15 m.

12-15 m.

See the rules in chapter 4's ninth simplified game for teams formed by two players. The main differences are that the number of players per team has increased here from two to three, and the dimensions of the field are increased (to a square measuring 12 to 15 meters). The attacking three players have six possessions of the ball and aim to keep the ball for as long as possible. When the ball runs out or is pushed out of the playing area by the defenders, one of the two attackers should be replaced by the third one, up to now waiting outside the area. Keep track of the seconds the three attackers keep possession of the ball. If you have more than three teams, you can organize a tournament to establish the best team.

TRAINING OBJECTIVES

- Learn to consider and then make use of the space available in the depth of the field.
- As an attacker, learn to always position yourself in a triangular formation to ensure there are two options for passing.
- Be able to disguise the direction of your pass.
- Develop sufficient speed of the ball when passing.

- Know when to pass and when not to pass.
- Learn to look out systematically for the 2-on-1 situation.
- Remember to lift the head while dribbling the ball.
- Learn to run in an uncontrolled space immediately after a successful pass.
- If there is a pressing defense, learn to use direct or wall passes.
- As defenders, learn to constantly diminish the space and time available to the three attackers and to anticipate their play, especially in the depth of the field.

CORRECTIVE EXERCISES

Use the ninth simplified game for 2 on 1 (in chapter 4), the first six simplified games in this chapter, and the "Passing, Receiving, and Shooting Games" (see chapter 3).

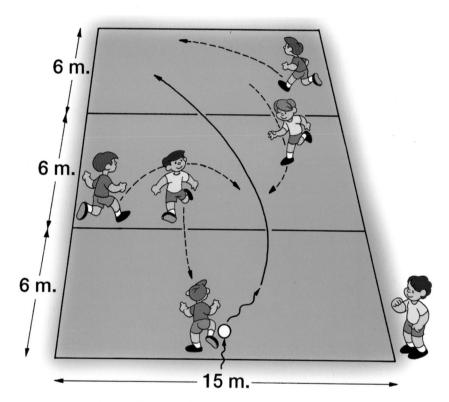

VARIATIONS

➤ This variation applies to more advanced players. Mark off a playing area 15 meters wide and 18 meters deep, separated into three zones of 6 meters each. The players are three attackers, two defenders, and one substitute for a defender. The more experienced the players are, the less wide and deep the area of play. One zone is assigned to each of the three attackers. Without being allowed to leave their assigned area, they try to keep possession against the two defenders, who may play in any of the three areas. Initially, none of the defenders is situated in the first attacker's zone. But immediately after the attacker touches the ball, both defenders may press him. When one of the defenders tackles successfully and manages to touch the ball three consecutive times, or when the ball runs out of play, the substitute (who should track the time with a stopwatch) moves into the playing area and replaces one of the defenders. With every attempt, the three attackers should try to keep the ball for 10 (or, later, for 15) seconds. The winning team is the one that keeps the ball the most times for 10 (15) seconds within 10 attempts.

➤ If only five players are available, the successful defender changes position and function with the attacker who failed.

8th Simplified Game
2 on 2 With Passes to Teammate

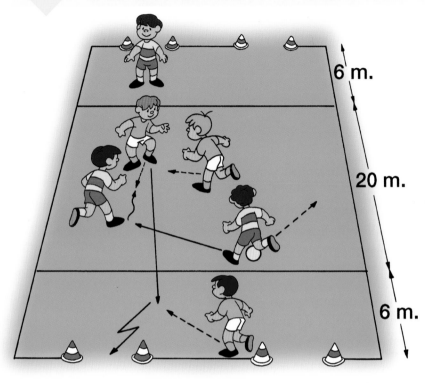

6 m.

20 m.

6 m.

Use a mini-soccer field, starting the game with a ball toss into the center of the field. Form two teams of three players. The two midfield players of each team try to gain possession of the ball and then to pass it to their teammate standing inside the opposing shooting zone. He or she may not leave the assigned zone. At first, do not allow any of the other players to enter the shooting area. Once the players fully understood the game, the "midfielders" may enter to support their "outlet" player or, when on the opponent's side, to tackle the "outlet" opponent while she is receiving or

Logical Progression of Games

Using the following progression of activities helps youngsters develop their capacity for executing passes deep into the field:

1. 2 on 2 with long through passes to one of the two attackers on the mini-soccer field.

2. 2 on 2 with long passes to one attacker.

3. 3 on 3 with long passes to one of the two attackers.

4. 3 on 3 with long passes to one attacker.

5. Long passes to one attacker shadowed by a defender (see the Third Simplified Game for teams formed by four players in chapter 7).

6. Free kick to a marked attacker (see Eighth Simplified Game for teams formed by two players, chapter 4).

7. Variation of the Seventh Simplified Game: "Maintaining Ball Possession 3 on 2" (in three separated areas).

8. Variation of the Seventh Simplified Game: "Long Passes Out of the Midfield" in chapter 7.

9. Long, direct passes to one attacker closely marked in the shooting zone of the mini-soccer field.

trying to score (with or without the teammates' help). After one attacker manages to score two goals, he or she has to rotate position and function with a teammate. Restart the game by one midfielder using a free kick from the edge of the shooting zone to the other midfield player—but never with a direct through pass to the outlet player in the opposite shooting area.

If there are eight players available, each team has three players in the midfield.

VARIATION

➤ The winning team is the one that keeps possession of the ball longer. No goals are scored.

TRAINING OBJECTIVES

- As a passer, learn to communicate and establish visual agreement with the receiver; pass the ball exactly when the receiver is ready.
- Be able to disguise the direction of the pass.
- As defender, don't allow the attacker sufficient time to think and prepare his play.
- Learn to anticipate or read the opponent's play.

CORRECTIVE EXERCISES

Use the fifth, ninth, and tenth simplified games for two-player teams (chapter 4) as well as Test 3 of the decathlon to improve the reach of defenders and teach them to disguise the direction of the pass.

9th Simplified Game
3 on 3 With Two Wide Goals

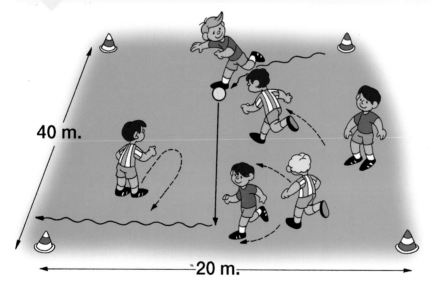

40 m.

20 m.

Players use half of a 7-on-7 soccer field, playing between one end line and the centerline. Set up goals on both lines (see illustration for the dimensions and placement). To score, an attacker must dribble the ball under control across the opponent's goal line, which is the width of the field.

Duration of the game: four periods of 3 minutes each.

VARIATIONS

➤ After controlling the ball across the opposing goal line, the attackers have to conclude their attack with an immediate shot on a soccer goal 11 meters behind it and defended by a neutral goalkeeper.

➤ The same game can be played with four goals (each 5 meters wide), two of them placed on each goal line separated by a distance of 20 meters. To score, the attackers have to either dribble or shoot the ball into one of the opposing goals.

TRAINING OBJECTIVES

In attacking, players work toward these goals:

- To know what to do when you are not in possession of the ball: that is, make yourself available for a pass in an area that is not controlled by the defending side. This way, the player in possession of the ball has the choice to either penetrate in the space that the attacker has created or pass.
- To attack in a triangular formation, ensuring width and depth.
- While dribbling the ball, to observe the behavior of both opponents and teammates so be able to make good decisions.
- To avoid revealing the next move.
- To take responsibility for each attacking move; any mistake may result in a goal for the opponents.

In defending, players work toward these goals:

- No player rests on the defense; on the contrary, they all participate fully in attack as well as in defense so that three defenders are always active.
- To ensure width in the defense, covering the whole width of the goal.
- To make sure cover is always provided for the player who is tackling a ball carrier by defending in a triangular formation.
- To channel the attack into the direction you want and then keep the ball in this area, crowding it also with your team's other defenders.
- To delay tackling as necessary, until being sure of receiving support from a teammate.
- After each conclusion of the opposing attack, remembering to complete the defense at the opposite side (concentrate on your task).
- To be able to take free kicks quickly and before the opponent defenders can build a "wall" in front of one end line.
- To initiate a counterattack quickly, with or without the help of the other teammates.
- To disguise the direction of any long pass.

CORRECTIVE EXERCISES

Choose from any of the earlier simplified games.

10th Simplified Game
3 on 3 With Passes Through Any of Four Goals

Use half of the 7-on-7 soccer field, placing four goals (each 2 meters wide) 5 meters inside the field (see illustration). After a ball toss into the center of the field, the players of both teams try to pass the ball to another teammate—*through one of the four goals*. Any

reception of the ball behind a goal but still inside of the playing area is considered good for a point. Scoring twice in a row in the same goal is not allowed. All free kicks must be taken from a distance at least 5 meters away from the nearest goal. After every two goals scored, all players rest for 2 minutes; during the rest they discuss their positive and negative actions of play.

VARIATIONS

➤ A neutral player plays with whatever team is in possession of the ball.

➤ Instead of passing, dribble the ball through any of the four goals.

The game can also be played on a mini-soccer field with the objective to score in any of the four goals from any area in the center of the field.

TRAINING OBJECTIVES

- Improve in the play without the ball; cooperate with teammates, adjusting to their behaviors.
- Be able to frequently change the speed and direction of your run (with the ball as well as without it) to gain some time and space for the next move.
- Run into the space behind the defenders and look out for the less-defended goal (it's imperative to move out of position after a successful pass).
- Reduce the dribble to a minimum, and move the ball quickly at your side with hard passes.
- Play direct or wall passes as required.

CORRECTIVE EXERCISES

See the previous simplified games.

11th Simplified Game
Centering the Ball

Using cones, divide a 7-on-7 soccer field into three corridors, the two lateral ones 10 meters wide and the central one about 25 meters wide. Each team attacks one goal; one of the team's players should be in the right-wing and another in the left-wing position, while the third player enters the central corridor. Both center forwards pass the ball to one of their wings, who must receive it within her zone. After having controlled the ball, the wing advances without any opposition until he or she arrives more or less level with the penalty area, where she centers the ball to the center forward, who followed in the central corridor. The opposite wing also should follow in her corridor. This wing, once level with the area, may run out of his corridor and position himself for executing a head kick from in front of the second goalpost. The center forward, however, occupies the zone in front of the first goalpost. Both teams practice in the same attacking formation for at least 3 minutes. Then the places are switched until everybody has played in all three positions. As a next step, hold a competition, in which the team scoring more goals—with a header—out of 10 attacks wins. The competition is over when all players have performed 10 times in the center forward position.

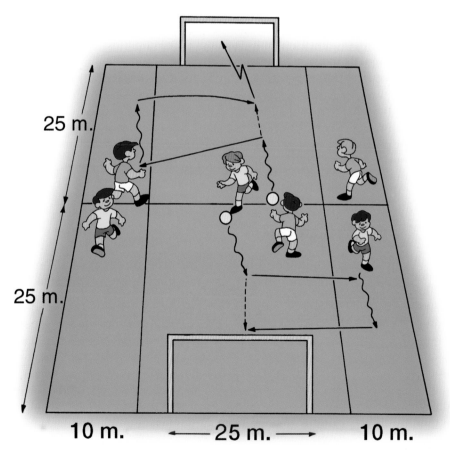

25 m.

25 m.

10 m.   ◄— 25 m. —►   10 m.

VARIATIONS

➤ Players use gymnastic balls or No. 3 balls to facilitate the execution of accurate centers and head kicks.

➤ The coach permits the wing to center the ball when stationary before centering with the ball on the run.

➤ A goalkeeper is included in the game, but may play only from (remaining on) the goal line.

➤ The goalkeeper plays with no special restrictions imposed.

➤ More experienced players practice this game with a defender who marks one of the other two attackers. The wing must therefore decide to which attacker he should center the ball: to the center forward or the wing of the opposite side.

TRAINING OBJECTIVES

- Learn to center the ball.
- Gain experience in the head kick.
- Learn to assume an optimal position in front of the goal before executing the head kick.
- Learn to run toward the oncoming ball before executing a head kick.

CORRECTIVE EXERCISES

See the first two variations, which are helpful remedial activities.

Level 3 Competitions

The 4-on-4 Triathlon and soccer competitions further develop the innate potential of players 10 years and older.

4-on-4 Triathlon

Include the triathlon periodically in the training program to enhance players' abilities to read and react to more complex situations and to an increased number of players. In the schedule here, "Europe" takes on "Asia" until a winner is decided. The following simplified games make up the 4-on-4 Triathlon.

Europe against Asia

Teams	China	Saudi Arabia	Thailand
Names of players			

Teams	Scotland	Sweden	Russia
Names of players			

First game: Dribble across the opponent's end line (3 × 3 min.)

Scores:

CHI-SCO	
SA-SWE	
THA-RUS	

Second game: Long passes out of the midfield (3 × 3 min.)

Scores:

CHI-SWE	
SA-RUS	
THA-SCO	

Third game: Score, defend, and counterattack (4 × 3 min.)

Scores:

CHI-RUS	
SA-SCO	
THA-SWE	

Final result: Europe against Asia _____ _____
(sum of victories)

Duration of the triathlon tournament: 2 hours and 15 minutes

Technical delegate: _____

Note: During the triathlon, changing the composition of the team is not permitted.

Organization of the 4-on-4 triathlon.

1. Dribble Across the Opponents' End Line

Two teams of four players each use half of a soccer field, playing between the end line and the centerline. Both teams try to control the ball to any spot of the opponent's end line. The game starts with a ball toss to the center. Players must be positioned at least 4.5 meters from the end line for free kicks and throw-ins.

Duration of the game: three periods of 5 minutes each.

2. Long Passes out of the Midfield

This game, too, is played on a soccer field between one offside line and the centerline. On each end line of this field you should use cones to mark off a 3-meter-wide goal, set 13 meters from each goalpost (see illustration). Two teams play in the midfield. Start the play with a ball toss. Without leaving the area of the midfield, each team tries to pass the ball through one of the opponent's two goals. It's a good idea to have plenty of reserve balls to assure effective practice.

Duration of the game: three periods of 3 minutes each.

3 m.

25 m.

3 m.

13 m.　　　　13 m.

3. Score, Defend, and Counterattack

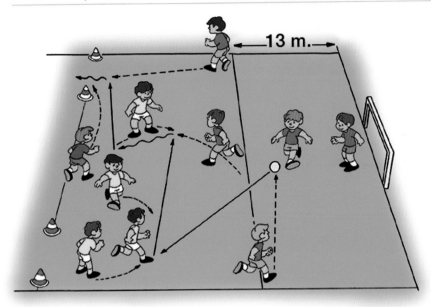

Again use just half of the 7-on-7 soccer field, setting up two extra goal areas with cones set in the wing positions on the centerline. Start the play with ball toss in the center. One team attacks the regular goal; the other team defends it and attacks the two goals in the wing positions on the centerline. The defenders score with a long pass through one of these two goals.

For all other rules, please consult and use the soccer rules given in the next section of this chapter. It works best to use a neutral goalkeeper in the regular goal area (see illustration). After every 3 minutes, the attackers and defenders should switch positions and functions.

Duration of the game: four periods of 3 minutes each.

7-on-7 Soccer

These are the rules that apply to the 7-on-7 game. If a rule is not specified here for some situation you and your players face in the game, the official rules of the game of soccer should apply.

Playing Field

The 7-on-7 field is a rectangle measuring 50 to 65 meters in length and 30 to 45 meters in width. This size allows you to fit three of these fields into one regular-sized soccer field. All other measurements are given in the diagram.

The field's dimensions are adapted to the physiological characteristics of young soccer players. In fact, the measurements take into account all aspects of the game including these:

1. Physical Preparation

   ➤ Most of the playing workout is aerobic.

   ➤ Frequent, short runs are characteristic, either with or without changes of direction and rhythm, jumps, and sudden stops.

   ➤ More demands are made on the young players' coordination capacities.

2. Technical Preparation

   ➤ The players have frequent contact with the ball, which benefits their developing basic skills.

   ➤ Because players are exposed to less complex game situations, their self-confidence grows, which results in their taking more initiative and using their innate capacity for imagination and creativity.

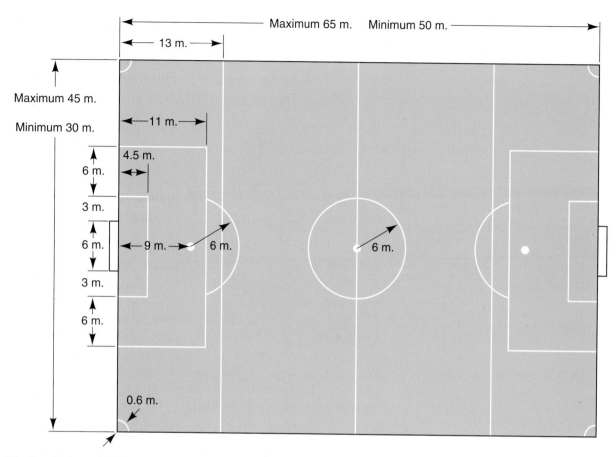

The 7-on-7 playing field. Three of these fields fit into one regular-sized soccer field.

> ➤ This version of soccer includes frequent occurrences of the basic and standard game situations, such as shooting a goal from any distance or angle or the systematic use of the 2-on-1 situation in attack.

3. Tactical Preparation

> ➤ In defense, because of the shorter distances between the players, it is easier for them to cover defense.

> ➤ In offense, players frequently change the front of the attack, use more wall or first-time passes, and attack more from the second line.

> ➤ The shorter distances allow players to gain valuable experiences in such standard situations as corners, throw-ins, free kicks, and penalties.

> ➤ Communication skills and cooperation are acquired under ideal conditions.

4. Dimensions of the Goals

> ➤ Young goalkeepers benefit more than any other players from the ideally sized goals in the 7-on-7 competition. When they defend a goal measuring 7.32 by 2.44 meters, goalkeepers often worry about any shot at goal, but defending the smaller goal areas (6 by 2 meters), better adapted to the heights of young players, they are more confident of saving the shot. Being exposed to less stress benefits their performances and enjoyment. When youngsters use traditional-size goals, the goalkeepers are often the big losers; due to the enormous size of the goal, only very rarely can they show their real talent. Having to defend

goals made to fit adult heights when they are still only 1.25 to 1.40 meters (about 4 to 5 feet) tall has turned many otherwise enthusiastic young goal-keepers into field players or even to another sport. In contrast, when the young goalkeepers defend a 7-on-7 soccer goal, their percentages of successful actions go up, even if they concede more goals at the end of these shorter games than in the traditional 11-on-11 game. Thanks to their more intensive involvement in the 7-on-7 games (a much higher rate of ball touches), the youngsters' learning benefits.

Size of the Ball

Players must use a No. 4 ball in the 7-on-7 game. Its circumference must measure between 63.5 (minimum) and 66 (maximum) centimeters. The ball's weight at the start of the game should be between 340 and 390 grams.

Using a ball adapted in size and weight to the heights and physical capacities of young players is imperative for learning to maneuver the ball well for these reasons:

➤ It facilitates the pass and the shot at goal (because the size and weight of the ball are adapted to the smaller foot and lesser power of younger players).

➤ Young players need not lift their foot excessively to dribble or receive the ball (therefore, they can remain in balance).

➤ In beating an opponent or executing dummies, youngsters are encouraged (by the smaller size of the ball) to move the foot above the ball or to pass it between the legs of the opponent.

© Joe Robbins

The smaller size of the 7-on-7 soccer field facilitates cooperation and communication among players.

➤ They avoid developing some bad habits caused by using the traditional soccer ball (with the official ball, young players generally use the foot tip to execute long clearances or shots at goal, many of them thereby falling into a bad habit that will be difficult to eradicate later).

➤ Using a No. 4 ball encourages young players to use headers ("kick" the ball with their heads) more frequently. The use of this ball also drastically improves technique, because players aren't afraid and usually don't close their eyes at the instant of impact.

➤ Using a No. 4 ball allows the ball carrier to consider all teammates for a pass, including the one farthest away. This helps improve the perception capacities.

Number of Players

The competition is played by two teams composed of 9 (minimum) or 10 (maximum) players. Only 7 members of one team, however, may play at the same time on the field, one of them defending the goal.

At least 5 players per team must be present to start the game. After the initiation of the match, the other players can join in. The 2 or 3 reserve players may substitute at any time for a player who is on the field, provided the substitution of players takes place level with the centerline but not when free kicks or penalties are awarded. The only exception is the rule that a substituted player may return to the playing field as often as the coach considers it convenient. During a match, if one team for any circumstances, including expulsions by the referee, should remain with fewer than 5 players, the referee concludes the match and declares the team with too few players as 0:3 losers.

Duration

Two periods of 25 minutes, with 5 minutes' halftime; if you hold a tournament in which several matches are played on the same day, reduce the duration of the matches to two periods of 20 minutes each.

Offsides and Free Kicks

In addition to the official offside rule, in a 7-on-7 soccer game a player has to be inside the 13-meter zone of the opposing team to be considered in an offside position. All other criteria for an offside stated in the official rules remain valid. All infringements of the rules are penalized with direct free kicks.

Referees

To encourage interest among youngsters in becoming referees, it's helpful to use only referees who are younger than 18 years of age for 7-on-7 soccer matches. This referee applies the rules just stated, and must be quite familiar with them.

This chapter presents youth coaches with a rich and varied program for children 10 years and up; its application allows kids to play tailor-made competitions and 7-on-7 soccer not only with pleasure and fun but also with success. With fewer players on a team, smaller playing areas, a variety of simplified games and competitions, and using lighter (No. 4) balls, all the boys and girls of this age group can feel capable of meeting the demands of a 7-on-7 game. Coaches observe through experience how the simplified games recommended for this age group reappear, one after another, in more complex situations in the 7-on-7 game. Playing 7-on-7 soccer well is a result of having understood and more or less mastered all these games and the ones in the 4-on-4 triathlon.

6

Developing Young Goalkeepers
Level 3

"Tomorrow's success is founded
on today's preparation."
Sir William Osler

Because few coaches have played as goalkeepers, their knowledge of how to train them is somewhat limited. Relatively few coaches give sufficient attention to the teaching and learning processes for this most important player of the team—even though everybody knows that winning or losing a match depends in many cases on the goalkeeper's performance. Whereas other team members can compensate for the errors of a field player, a mistake made by the goalkeeper usually results in a goal.

Although modern soccer demands good all-around skills from all players, the goalkeeper must be treated as the only *specialist* on the team. In contrast to other team members, the goalkeeper covers a very limited territory and is the only player allowed to play the ball with the hands. Due to the goalkeeper's specific function and importance as a key player in any soccer team, special attention and great importance should be given to his or her development.

Profile of a Goalkeeper

The great influence of a goalkeeper's performance on the result of the game often puts the player in the center of decisive game situations and important discussions. After a fine performance everybody congratulates him or her, but if the performance wasn't satisfactory or was poor, the goalkeeper receives severe reprimands. That is why a goalkeeper must be a serene person! The player should be confident about his or her abilities and capacities, building constantly on this self-confidence through positive self-talk and frequent training.

A goalkeeper should express or radiate calmness and confidence during the game to other team members, thus positively influencing their performance level. On the other hand, the goalkeeper's having a strong personality and self-confidence can negatively condition the opponents who, during the conclusion of their attacks, might focus too much of their attention on his or her play.

When the goalkeeper is insecure, shows nerves, or is slow in the decision-making process, this poor quality of play undoubtedly influences his or her own team negatively. The team's defenders, as well as its attackers, will likely risk less in offense and be afraid to attack with more than four players nearby.

Just these few comments explain why any average team with an excellent goalkeeper can win or at least tie the match against a much stronger team with a less skillful goalie. And to successfully fulfill the important tasks in the game, the goalkeeper must have certain psycho-physical capacities that differ from those of the field players.

"The ability to relax under pressure is often a vital factor in competition."

L. Morehouse/L. Gross

Speed

The most important physical capacity for a goalkeeper is speed—speed in reaction, acceleration, power, and limb movements. A satisfactory level of all these qualities allow the player, for instance, to stop balls shot at more than 130 kilometers per hour (about 80 miles per hour) or to close down an attacker who approaches the goal with the ball under control. But speed is not the only physical capacity to take into consideration. It should be combined with excellent coordination and flexibility, along with the other qualities described in this chapter.

Speed is the most important quality in a goalkeeper.

Accurate Decisions

To be able to benefit from the different qualities of speed, it's imperative that the goalkeeper effectively uses whatever information is available prior to the opponent's shot on goal. In other words, anticipating the eventual outcome from early components of the opponent's move is an integral part of a goalkeeper's successful performance.

This player must have an excellent knowledge and understanding of what is going on in the game as the basis for his or her perceptions. *What a goalkeeper can "read" or perceive determines how he or she should act.* The more experience and knowledge the goalkeeper has gained, the more he is able to focus his visual attention on the most relevant sources of information. Expert keepers have developed a better visual search strategy than young ones have, who usually watch only the ball and are less aware of the position and movements of the players off the ball. Therefore, as a coach you play an important part in the learning process as you try to direct the learner's attention to relevant sources of information.

Considering that more than half of the job of a keeper is mental conditioning and judgment (which both come from experience), it's understandable that most of the errors among young players are caused less by their technical level of play than by weak or incorrect decision making.

Technically well-prepared goalkeepers who are physically fit still must be trained to become excellent decision makers who know what is best to do in a particular game situation. Their errors in making decisions are caused either by poor attention, poor perception, a lack of determination, or a lack of knowledge (from poor-quality coaching sessions). It's fundamental that young players learn to use their brains to quickly process all relevant information, with the aim to select the best motor response possible to execute—thanks to having already developed a high level of physical fitness.

For goalkeepers, a tactical training has to be considered as important as a technical preparation. The older the goalkeeper, the more that tactical training should replace technical work (in which no decision making is required initially).

Goalkeepers from 14 years and up should be systematically exposed to a great variety of problems that are included in simplified games specifically designed to improve their performance. Through these games they learn to choose the most effective response among several possibilities.

Courage

Another important aspect of the goalkeeper's performance, besides staying calm (a characteristic based on self-confidence) and being aggressive as necessary in a given moment, is having courage combined with determination. Being courageous is imperative, especially in 1-on-1 situations, during shots executed from short distances and during corners.

The goalkeeper's capacity to control the arousal level will minimize errors. Studies have demonstrated that performance deteriorates under high levels of arousal; this is especially true of cognitive performance, which includes problem solving and decision making. Every goalkeeper is exposed to high levels of stress some 15 to 25 times during a game; the player is aware that any small mistake or bad judgment can dramatically change the outcome of the competition. In other words, everybody expects him or her to be a perfect player, and the goalie has to live with this expectation.

To overcome this challenge the goalie should be a master of "the inner game of soccer," which involves positive self-talk (for example, "Today's my day!" or "I'm the greatest!" or "Nobody can score against me."). Nevertheless, when the ball is far away, it's advisable for the goalkeeper to execute in front of the goal some fundamental technical or warm-up drills that keep him or her physically and mentally ready for the next decisive action.

Tips for Training Goalkeepers

To optimize performance, it's effective to have all goalkeepers play a different position frequently, one outside of the goal area, during the training sessions. This will help them develop in the psychological and physical areas they need to perform well. Furthermore they experience the sort of tension attackers feel and the difficulties they face when trying to overcome the last player of the opponent's defense. The experiences gained when playing as defender or attacker allow goalkeepers to perform with greater success. Goalkeepers who in their first six years have played mini-soccer (with two goals to be defended simultaneously), 7-on-7, and 8-on-8 soccer before moving to the 11-on-11 competition have a higher level of perception and greater knowledge than traditionally trained goalkeepers.

Furthermore, thanks to the logical progression of the competitions in which they play an ever more active role, they become mentally quicker and know how to anticipate the opponent's play much better than those who have only been exposed to a traditional training program based mainly on acquiring technical skills.

Ideally, a goalkeeper's specific training is directed and supervised by a specialist goalkeeper coach, usually a former, experienced goalkeeper. However, in most of these cases, the goalkeeper coach doesn't know how to link the coaching of the goalkeeper with that of the defenders—an important task now that goalkeepers are more than ever part of the whole defense.

When a specialist coach trains a pupil with a variety of exercises and games in which the young goalkeeper must solve the common problems of competitions, the youngster acquires a broad knowledge and experience that allow him or her to select the most appropriate technique. The young player also learns to execute skills correctly with requisite speed, flexibility of the muscles, and mobility in the joints.

Furthermore such a young goalkeeper learns to command and lead teammates with an authoritative voice. The clarity and brevity of his or her directions ("It's mine!" "Leave it!" "Out!") are imperative for creating the desired effect. Last, but not least, the aspiring goalie learns to encourage teammates with positive comments.

Unfortunately it's not unusual to see many young players, still limited in their performance outside of the goal, suddenly decide to become goalkeepers. Coaches should encourage players to become goalies only when they display a certain natural talent for this particular position. Only those young players succeed who bring to the position a certain basic level of most of the capacities that make a good goalkeeper.

The road to success has very few travelers because many get lost trying to find short cuts.

Development Model for Goalkeepers

The development model for goalkeepers consists of four levels. The diagram on page 154 illustrates each level and its divisions.

Basic Stance

The basic stance is the ready position that goalkeepers assume before their interventions. The following tips will help increase the young goalkeeper's success. Goalkeepers should learn these principles:

➤ Always initiate the movement from "tiptoe" (on the balls of feet) position.

➤ Maintain balance, ensuring it through the feet positioned shoulder width apart. Raise the arms and hands about the waist.

➤ Keep the weight of the body equally distributed between both legs to avoid finding yourself surprised to be on the "wrong foot."

➤ Keep the knees forward of the toes.

➤ Bend the knees slightly to be ready to spring (the upper leg and tibia should form an angle of 110 to 120 degrees).

➤ Maintain good balance, with the trunk inclined slightly forward.

➤ Draw the attention mainly to the ball but also stay aware of the positions of teammates and opponents.

➤ Relax when the ball is being played more than 40 meters away from the goal, assuming the basic position just immediately before a shot could be made.

Level 1
Exercises and games with or without one attacker (Learning of fundamental skills in foreseen situations)

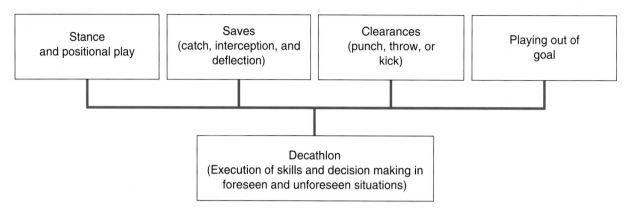

| Stance and positional play | Saves (catch, interception, and deflection) | Clearances (punch, throw, or kick) | Playing out of goal |

Decathlon
(Execution of skills and decision making in foreseen and unforeseen situations)

Level 2
Exercises and games with two or more attackers (Consolidation of skills and decision making in modified situations)

| Stance and positional play | Saves (catch, interception, and deflection) | Clearances (punch, throw, or kick) | Playing out of goal |

Level 3
Exercises and games with attackers and help of one or two defenders
(Improvement of skills and decision making in foreseen and unforeseen situations)

| Stance and positional play | Saves (catch, interception, and deflection) | Clearances (punch, throw, or kick) | Playing out of goal |

Level 4
Simplified games that frequently involve the goalkeeper
(Mastery, execution, and correct decision making in unforeseen situations)

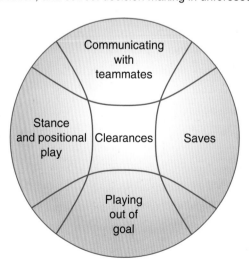

The development model for goalkeepers.

Positional Play

One ability that is vital for goalkeepers to develop is to get positioned before a shot at goal is made in such a way that they can intercept the ball within a minimum range of movement. Finding the best possible position in relation to both the attacker with the ball and the goalposts helps goalies cut down the number of desperate saves and last-second moves. When good goalkeepers play, it seems as though the balls always come straight to them. Every one of their saves looks easy. Goalkeepers who frequently execute acrobatic dives are not the best ones because their positional play is at fault. On the contrary, experienced keepers, conditioned by their fine positional play, hardly need to dive or leap.

Many goalkeepers feel most comfortable standing on or very close to the goal line. However, there are increasing situations in today's games that oblige them to master the game off the line as well and sometimes to act as sweeper.

In general, a goalkeeper initiates an intervention from the line that divides the angle formed by the triangle of the ball and the two goalposts. When moving forward on this imaginary line toward the attacker in possession of the ball, the goalkeeper finally reaches that point at which he can cover the whole shooting angle without having to execute a save using a maximal range of movement or extension of the arms or legs. The closer he comes to the opponent who prepares the shot at goal, the less time and less angle are available for scoring. But the more the goalie moves away from the line bisecting that angle, the less his intervention is likely to succeed.

Exercises for Stance and Positional Play

1. This exercise helps inexperienced goalkeepers mentally visualize the triad between the three points formed by goalposts and the attacker with the ball. As coach, position yourself anywhere on the 11-meter line (on a 7-on-7 soccer field) or the 16.5-meter line (on a full regulation field). Two cords (long pieces of rope) should be tied to the goalposts, one at the right goalpost and the other at the left, and tied to your right ankle. Depending on how the coach moves along the 11- or 16.5-meter line, the goalkeeper modifies his position. He tries to always remain on the (imaginary) line bisecting the shooting angle, and must come far enough forward to be able to reach with his right foot, without difficulty, to the right rope or with his left foot to the left rope. At the same time, his hands should reach out to control the space to both his sides. If he cannot reach both ropes with his feet, he knows that he is badly positioned, which would allow the attacker enough of a gap to score.

2. One player dribbles the ball along the lines of the penalty area, frequently changing his direction. The goalkeeper, meanwhile, assumes a ready position about 3 meters outside the goal and always positioned on the line that bisects the shooting angle, also moving according to the direction and speed of the attacker. The goalkeeper's coach should position himself behind the net to carefully observe and analyze the positional play of the goalie and correct this playing position whenever necessary.

3. Set out five balls no further than 2 meters inside the penalty area (see illustration). One player strikes them all, one after another, into the goal. To allow the goalie sufficient time to choose an advantageous position for play and assume a correct basic position, the attacker, after every shot at goal, has to run out of the penalty area before being allowed to take on the next ball.

VARIATION

➤ Assign the same exercise with a second attacker positioned close (about 5 to 6 meters) to the goalkeeper. His primary function is to pick up the rebounds from the goalie or from the posts, but from his position in front of the goal he may also deflect the shot at goal directly into the net.

4. Two attackers at the edge of the penalty area pass the ball to each other across distances of between 8 and 12 meters. Meanwhile, the goalkeeper has to adapt his position in the goal to the changing position of the ball. One of the two attackers should try "all of a sudden" to surprise him with a shot before he can assume an optimal position to save the ball.

5. Four players work with the goalkeeper in this activity. One attacker on either side of the goal passes the ball from the end line to one of his teammates on the line of the penalty area. The player who receives the ball may score with a first-time shot or she may instead pass it back to the end line or to one side where her teammate, always at least 8 meters from the passer, could receive the ball. The idea is for any attacker to surprise the goalkeeper with a shot. The aim of the goalkeeper in all phases of this exercise, however, is to demonstrate correct positional play, allowing him to narrow the angle for any shot at goal.

6. As coach, you should stay behind the goal to observe the play. Give a visual signal to one of the six players, situated in different attacking positions on the 11-meter (or 16.5-meter) line. Then this player tries to score quickly with a shot. Give the goalkeeper feedback on any problems in positional play that you observe from your post behind the goal. The goalie's aim is to always position himself, at the instant any shot is made at goal, on the line bisecting the shooting angle. This task becomes easier when all attackers face the centerline. So after the coach calls a player's name, that attacker turns around and shoots so quickly at goal that the goalkeeper has hardly any time to position himself correctly in the goal area or to assume an optimal, basic ready position. As a goalie improves, you can diminish the goalkeeper's time further by calling out the attackers' names at shorter intervals.

7. Six players are situated around the center circle of the soccer field with a diameter of 18.3 meters. Their aim is to pass the ball from outside the circle through any of the three 6-meter gates established in the center of the circle in the form of a triangle (see illustration). A goalkeeper defends all three goals at the same time, moving from one goal cone to the other according to the position of the ball. Work with the goalie to always take small steps, while continuing to attentively watch the ball's trajectory; this technique allows the player to transfer his or her body weight easily from one leg to the other. The result should be an optimal positional play, preventing the six attackers from scoring goals. Clearly, the goalkeeper would not be able to adapt quickly enough to the demands of this game by using long steps or moves.

8. A right wing (or left wing) penetrates deeply into the opponent's half. After having dribbled the ball through a pair of cones, placed outside the penalty area and about 3 meters away from the end line, the wing may strike or pass the ball either to the center forward or to the left wing (right wing) who is in front of the second post. Whoever receives the pass tries to score with a first-time shot (a head kick or shot). In this exercise the goalkeeper must continually demonstrate an optimal level of positional work without coming fully out of the goal. When the goalie covers the angle of the right (left) wing's shot close to the nearby goalpost, his right (left) foot is already placed in such way that he can quickly cover the goal in case of a center. The wing never lets the goalkeeper know whether she will try to score, execute a dummy goal-shot, or center the ball. Only when the goalkeeper learns to quickly switch positions can he face both forward players and prevent a goal from being scored.

Exercises to Improve Reaction Speed

To improve the goalkeeper's reaction speed, it's recommended to use lighter balls, especially the No. 4 ball, with these exercises.

1. Two attackers stand on the line of the goalkeeper area, at both sides of the penalty point. Their objective is to deflect the shots that a third player executes from the edge of the penalty area into the goal. To surprise the goalkeeper, the third attacker may also shoot directly—without having the teammates divert the ball.

2. The coach shoots the ball at different speeds and heights into the goal, defended by a goalkeeper turned so that his or her *back* is facing the attacker (see illustration). Only when the coach calls the goalie may the player then turn around to fix the ball, save it, or clear it out of the area.

3. From a position behind the goal, you, as coach, visually signal one of three attackers, all in possession of a ball and all situated inside the penalty area at different distances from the goal. While the player you have signaled executes the shot, the goalie assumes an optimal, correct ready position to prevent the ball from going into the goal. Give the goalie feedback as necessary.

4. Stand behind the goal, ready to visually signal two attackers. The two players, each with a ball and situated about 35 meters from the goal, dribble with the same speed toward the penalty area. They should stay separated by at least 8 meters. When they come within about 20 meters of the goal, which is defended by a goalkeeper, let them know through a visible signal (which should be invisible to the goalie) to carry out the shot at goal from the penalty area line. One attacker shoots, while the other one goes for the rebound.

5. Use a 7-on-7 soccer goal, and position the goalie on the ground just beside a post outside it. One attacker dribbles the ball from 6 meters outside the penalty area, aiming to score from inside the area. When the player starts the individual attack, the goalkeeper gets up from the ground to position himself well in the goal and assume a basic ready position; he tries to carry out the save. The attacker (who also can be another goalkeeper) has four attempts to score without ever entering more than 2 meters into the penalty area. The goalkeeper should start twice from each goalpost.

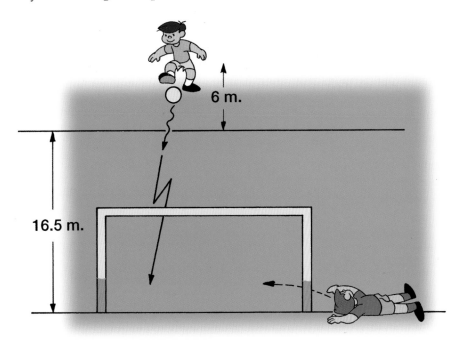

Saves

In soccer matches, the intervention that goalkeepers carry out most frequently is simply a catch. However, goalkeepers can also save the ball with an interception or deflection. In general, a goalkeeper can stop the ball with a catch (of either high or low incoming balls). He not only uses his hands, but also places an added barrier beyond the ball with his body and legs.

There are three golden rules for catching the ball in the air or on the ground:

1. Get the body behind the ball whenever possible.
2. Get the ball to the chest as it is caught.
3. Cushion the ball softly.

After a catch, with or without a leap, the ball remains in possession of the goalkeeper who continues play with an offensive action, for instance with an accurate throw or kick of the ball to one of his teammates.

If there isn't sufficient time to reach the ball with both hands, the goalkeeper intercepts the shot without controlling it. The techniques of interceptions and deflections over the bar or around the post are probably the most difficult ones for the goalie to master. Before the ball arrives level with the goalkeeper's body, the hand closest to the oncoming ball should meet it, with the leg of the same side being bent, regardless of whether the goalie intercepts or deflects the shot with a dive on the ground or in the air. Young goalkeepers often err by trying to stop low shots directed toward a corner

© Mary E. Messenger

After a successful catch, the goalkeeper can choose to throw or kick it to a teammate.

of the goal with the "opposite" (upper) hand. This mistake reduces the diving goalkeeper's reach considerably, and the player must then stretch out completely to intercept or deflect the ball around the post.

Unfortunately, many goalkeepers are trained in diving and catching low or high balls without the presence of teammates who might affect their play or even players who might be potential goal scorers. It's important to know that the performance of the goalkeeper and attackers improves little when stationary balls or balls in movement are simply shot at goal. To learn to anticipate the best possible interventions, the goalie needs to be exposed to real game situations during training. *It is the practice of game situations, in the presence of defenders and attackers and with the speed of competition, that best improves any goalkeeper's performance.* The goalkeeper learns to read the game, decide what technique to use, and when to interfere.

"No practice wastes talent."

Leonardo da Vinci

Consequently, exercises and games whose objective is to improve the techniques of saves (such as catching, intercepting, or deflecting the ball with or without a leap; being upright or obliged to dive) should not give the goalie advance knowledge of when, from where, or how the shot will be taken. By simulating real game situations, the goalkeeper is forced at the instant of the opponent's attack to find the best possible solution. After making the decision, he or she then acts accordingly, without any loss of time.

During practice, the coach must carefully observe how well the young goalie executes different goalkeeper techniques and tactical plays, evaluating performance and also noting whether the goalie and last defender demonstrate optimal communication and cooperation. To assure effective learning, the mistakes should be corrected *immediately* after their occurrences. During the process of the youngsters' learning from mistakes, the coach should remember also to praise the players!

Exercises to Improve Saving Technique

1. Shot With Opponent (1 on 1). See illustration and game 18 of the "Passing, Receiving, and Shooting Games" in chapter 3.

3 m.

VARIATIONS

➤ Use two defenders instead of one. The first closes down the attacker with the ball, and the second covers. See illustration and game 19 of the "Passing, Receiving, and Shooting Games" in chapter 3.

➤ Use a goalie and defender and two attackers. Play the game as 2 on 1, starting with a pass of one attacker from the end line to the teammate, who is situated on the 16.5-meter (or 11-meter) line. After the initial pass, one defender and the goalkeeper (both starting from the end line) try to prevent the shot's scoring.

2. Quick Shot (1 on 2). As coach, stand inside the penalty area to start. The coach quickly passes the ball from inside the penalty area to one of three players who are expecting it in different positions at the edge of the penalty area. All three players should be at least 5 meters away from each other. The one who receives the ball played by the coach tries to score a goal while the remaining two do everything they can to prevent his scoring.

3. Goalkeeper Plus 2 on 1. Two attackers, situated 8 meters outside the penalty area, try to overcome a defender and score in less than 8 seconds. The attack finishes with

- the ball's being out of the field,
- an infringement by the attackers or the defenders (penalty),
- an offside, or
- after 8 seconds.

The goalkeeper learns when to leave the goal line and when to remain in goal. As players improve, shorten the allotted time to 5 seconds.

VARIATION

➤ Three players start their attack from 25 meters in front of the goal, with the two defenders expecting them at the edge of the penalty area. The goalkeeper, besides showing a correct stance and good positional play at the instant of the shot, must decide whether to stay in goal or to run out of it. Subsequently, he has to select and execute the most effective defensive action to avoid a goal's being scored with the first or second shot (rebound).

25 m.

4. Goalkeeper Plus 4 on 2. This game involves four forwards against two defenders, as well as the goalie, on a 7-on-7 soccer field. The attack is initiated with a free kick on the centerline. The four forwards must score within 5 seconds (you can first specify 8 seconds), trying to avoid playing all in line and running into an offside position. Due to the numerical superiority of the attackers in relation to the defenders, the goalkeeper interferes frequently and, therefore, improves quickly.

Clearances (Punch, Kick, or Throw)

If the close presence of one or more opponents makes the goalkeeper forget to catch a high-flying ball with both arms, protecting it with his trunk, he should clear the ball with one or both fists. Sometimes external conditions, such as rain during the match or a wet field, should suggest that he not try to catch the slippery ball. When a ball is too difficult to catch because of its height or speed, or the presence of opponents, it's better to either punch it with one or both fists or clear the ball with a deflection over the bar or around the post.

In punching with the fists, bending and extending the arms quickly in the moment of impact, the goalkeeper's accuracy and power can clear the ball out of the reach of the opponents. The distance of the clearance depends on the power developed by the goalkeeper—as well as on the speed of the oncoming ball. The goalie first learns to punch the ball with both fists held together. Care should be taken that the thumbs are held outside the fists; otherwise a broken thumb could be the outcome.

Initially the goalkeeper is trained to punch the ball back into the same direction from which it came. Subsequently, the goalie learns to confront high-flying balls that come from either side. In this situation the player should always use the fist furthest away from the oncoming ball to clear it. For example, the goalkeeper should use his right fist when the center comes from the left, but use the left fist when the ball is centered from his right side.

Within a split second the goalkeeper must perceive the spot from where the ball is kicked; correctly assess its trajectory, spin, and speed; and determine whether to catch it, deflect it, or punch it. In this game situation, the goalkeeper's attention focuses mainly on the ball. He modifies his position in the small area, following the ball's trajectory, making sure that he only decides to rush out of goal when there's a good chance of catching or clearing the ball before anybody else can play it.

It's imperative, for playing outside the goal, that the goalkeeper "feel" the precise moment for rushing out of goal. Any mistake the goalie makes in assessing either the ball's speed, height, or trajectory or the opponent's running speed could result in a goal.

Clearance Exercises

Practicing game situations frequently can improve and train the goalkeeper's capacity to punch the ball with one or two fists, dive for it, catch it, or deflect it. Some good examples of true game situations later in this chapter are Test 6 of the Goalkeeper Decathlon, "Control of the Goalkeeper's Area" and "Accurate Clearances With Kicks" (see the Decathlon section). In chapter 7, the Twelfth Simplified Game, "4 on 2 With Head-Kicks," provides realistic training; practicing corners from either side (progressively increasing the number of attackers and defenders) is also helpful.

1. Long Clearances. The coach or an attacker plays balls at different speeds and heights from outside the penalty area to the goal. Depending on the characteristics of the shot at goal, the goalie saves and then clears the balls into a designated area of the field.

2. Clearance to the Side Lines. After having saved a shot at goal, the goalkeeper clears the ball as quickly as possible through one of two goals set up with cones on the sidelines of the penalty area on the left and right sides. The selection of the direction of the clearance depends on the play of the attacker, who, after his shot at goal from 16 meters, goes on to defend one of the goal areas.

VARIATION

➤ After the save, the goalie has to clear the ball within 3 seconds through one of three goals set up (with cones) inside the penalty area. Two attackers (one at 16 meter's distance and the other 11 meters away) try to prevent his scoring through one of the three goals, using any clearance technique.

3. Accurate Clearances With Five Attackers. Four attackers position themselves around the penalty area. A fifth one has possession of the ball and dribbles it close to the edge of the penalty area until he decides to execute a shot at goal through a gap created by his four teammates. While the goalkeeper interferes, all attackers go for a possible rebound, which must be taken within 3 seconds after the goalkeeper's first intervention. None of the attackers is allowed to deflect the initial shot at goal. Depending on the distance of the nearest attacker at the instant of his save, the goalkeeper decides what technique to use. It's important for the goalie to clear the ball to spaces that the five attackers are not covering, of course. For every clearance of the ball out of the penalty area, the goalie wins 1 point; the attackers can gain 2 points only with rebound goals and 1 point only with a direct goal. For any infringement committed by the goalie, a penalty is awarded the attackers. All five attackers may shoot the moving ball from the edge of the area as long as they don't miss the goal. If an attacker fails, however, she or he is replaced by another player. The game is over once all five players have been replaced.

VARIATIONS

➤ The coach doesn't allow the goalkeeper to block the shots at goal.

➤ Two defenders assist the goalie, looking for defensive rebounds. They interfere from a position close to both goalposts immediately after the shot on goal, clearing the ball out of the danger zone.

4. Clearances Against Three Attackers. Three players stand 30 meters in front of one goal, serving as attackers. Once they penetrate slightly into the penalty area (but not more than 2 meters), one of them shoots and the other two do everything they can to pick up the rebound. The goalkeeper, who may not block the ball, should clear it through a zone the attackers leave uncovered.

VARIATIONS

➤ The three attackers must face a defender in addition to the goalkeeper.

➤ Two defenders stand next to the goalposts and assist the goalkeeper in clearing the ball from the penalty area (defensive rebound).

Playing out of Goal

Game statistics show that a goalkeeper interferes not more than once in 3 minutes. Most of his interventions take place outside of the goal area, especially at center, when one attacker manages to control the ball in his area without any defender being able to interfere before the shot at goal and when the ball is played back to the goalie. Often an intervention occurs when the ball is loose in the penalty area due to a rebound from the post or any player's body or to a loss in the control of the ball by one of the defenders or an attacker.

In all these cases, the goalkeeper must decide in only a split second whether to rush out of goal or to remain close to the goal line. *If even the slightest possibility exists that another team defender could still prevent the attacker from taking a shot, the goalkeeper should stay in goal!* Once a goalie decides to run out to confront the situation 1 on 1, however, he or she should do it aggressively and with determination and not modify the play halfway.

In a 1-on-1 situation the goalkeeper must be prepared to find the correct response to the attacker's two possible actions: dribbling or shooting. The goalkeeper should narrow the shooting angle as well as possible through her run-out, but the player must also learn to hold back patiently, forcing the opponent into hurried actions or mistakes. In this response, the goalie should keep upright as long as possible, with arms stretched wide to reduce the ball carrier's vision and distract him. With this behavior the goalkeeper can easily adapt to the attacker's offensive actions and, by executing a dummy, even oblige the opponent into doing what she wants.

When an attacker tries to play the ball around her, the goalkeeper, after having sharply assessed the time and space parameters, may dive to block with determination or, even better, collect the rolling ball. But if the ball is out of the goalie's range of action, she should try to cover the shooting angle with a fine positional play.

During the run out, the goalie should accelerate as much as possible during the first meters, but then must slow down the running speed as she nears the attacker. Only this way can she react successfully in the basic ready position.

The farther she finds herself outside of goal, the more possibilities exist for the attacker to beat her, especially if she goes down too early, allowing the attacker to lift the ball over her outstretched body.

In playing the position, the goalkeeper must follow the same basic rule that guides other defense players for the team. Facing an opponent 1 on 1, the goalie must reduce the space and time available to the attacker as much as possible to force the opponent to speed up (and often, therefore, to commit errors). The less time and space that are available for the attacker, the better the chances for the goalkeeper to win the "duel."

Exercises for Playing out of Goal

1. Running out, Lying Down, and Stretching out in Front of the Ball. The goalkeeper rushes out with speed and aggressiveness. His aim is to lie down just in front of the stationary ball placed in different spots in front of the goal at a distance of 6 to 8 meters. While lying down and stretching out, the goalkeeper collects the ball with both hands. From his position behind the goal, the coach evaluates the goalkeeper's technique of running out and getting down, especially looking for these aspects:

- A quick approach in a straight line up to the stationary ball.

- Getting down quickly from a vertical into a horizontal position, so that an attacker would not be able to pass the ball below the goalie's body as he or she was lying down.

- Good positioning of the hands when collecting the ball on the ground.

2. Challenge With a Stationary Ball. Set a ball down on the ground in front of the goalkeeper's area, as in the illustration. One attacker gets on the edge of the penalty area, facing a goalkeeper positioned in the center of the goal. Give the players a visible signal for them to start. Both try to reach the ball first and then play it, but they have different objectives: one intends to score and the other one wants to clear the ball out of the penalty area. The goalkeeper, depending on the attacker's and his or her own speed, has to decide whether to kick the ball first or to hold back, covering the shooting angle of the attacker, by placing his or her body close to the ball, and thus forcing the attacker to try dribbling. If the attacker has been forced to a dribble, the goalie should get down, stretch out, and grip the moving ball as the opponent runs into range. It's useful if you, as coach, modify the ball's position inside the area—as well as the distances between the competitors—to give the players more experience in optical-motor assessment.

3. Challenge With the Moving Ball. An attacker pushes the ball from the edge of the penalty area some 6 to 8 meters into the area. The player then tries to control it again before the goalkeeper can do so. After assessing the speed of the ball, her distance to the attacker, and the speed of her opponent, the goalkeeper decides what to do. Remaining in goal is certainly a mistake. That is why she should choose between running out to block the shot or the dribble of the attacker and trying to clear the loose ball before the opponent can. By practicing this situation frequently, the goalkeeper can gain valuable experience in coping with loose balls in the penalty area.

4. Challenge in a Real 1-on-1 Situation. Situate an attacker on the edge of the penalty area and the goalkeeper on the goal line. At your signal, the attacker has 4 seconds in which to try to beat the goalkeeper with a dribble and score from any spot inside the goalkeeper's area.

VARIATIONS

➤ A wing passes the ball across the penalty area to another teammate, the attacker, situated on the edge of the "box." While the ball is on its way and the attacker is controlling the ball, the goalkeeper rushes out, trying to do whatever is possible to avoid a goal being scored with a shot or a successful dribbling. The goal must be scored within 5 seconds of the initial pass to count as a point.

➤ A midfielder passes the ball from different positions outside of the penalty area into a wide space between an attacker at the edge of the penalty box and the goalkeeper standing on the goal line. Both assess the situation with the intention to win the challenge.

5. The Sweat Box. Use cones to mark off a square that measures 6 meters on each side, and call on four attackers plus one goalie. The goalkeeper plays inside the square against an attacker who starts from a position 8 meters outside. To collect a point, the goalie must prevent the attacker from running—with the ball under control—across the square. If the attacker loses control of the ball or happens to play it across one of the sidelines, the goalkeeper wins the match. After the first player has attacked, the second, third, and fourth launch their individual attacks. The competition ends after 12 attacks, with every opponent player having attacked three times. Generally the goalkeeper should win more points than the attackers. The purpose of this exercise is that the goalie will learn from it to condition the opponent's play through the application of a body feint. Convincing someone of a feint only works when the maneuver is executed in time and when the attacker is about 3 to 4 meters in front of the goalie.

6. Twice 2 on 1. Designate the playing area with cones as shown in the illustration, and use two attackers, one defender, and one goalie. The attackers first face the defender at the 10-meter line. After having played out the first defender and controlled the ball in the first wide goal, the two attackers take on the second defender, who is the goalkeeper. He defends the second goal, set 10 meters behind the first one, but should move out of goal only after the ball has been controlled in the first one. To beat the goalkeeper and score a valid goal, one of the two attackers must control the ball on the second goal line without having been in an offside position during the development of the attack.

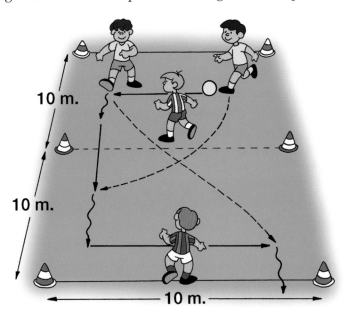

7. Dribbling Across the Opponent's End Line. This is a variant of the Sixth Simplified Game for 4 on 4 (in chapter 7), so you should use its rules and setup with the players. Consult the illustration here as well for setting up the field and play. In this variation one field player of each team becomes a goalkeeper. The goalies may play in any part of the field and may use their hands.

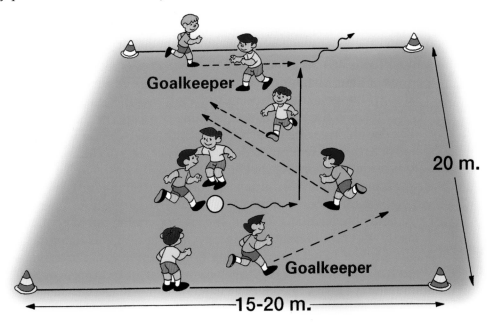

Common Mistakes Playing out of Goal

These are the most frequently encountered errors in playing outside of the goal area:

- Remaining on the goal line instead of running out aggressively to encounter the attacker in possession of the ball.
- Exiting although a teammate still can interfere before the shot at goal is to be taken.
- Not establishing good communication and cooperation with other defenders, resulting in a poor synchronization of actions between the goalkeeper and defenders.
- Approaching the attacker with too much speed, instead of slowing down as the goalie is about 5 meters from the attacker. When the goalie reaches an attacker who is still on the run, the attacker has no problem in beating or passing him or her with ease.
- Clearing the ball but without accuracy (perhaps even to an opponent) and without power (not sending it far away enough from the goal, so that the ball may return in a few seconds).
- Going down on the ground too frequently, almost like a habit, instead of remaining upright and in a balanced position.
- Going down into a sitting position instead of down toward one side.
- Tackling the attacker feet first while going down.
- Losing contact with the goal when rushing out to one side to an attacker who has a narrow shooting angle—instead of remaining in goal, covering the shooting angle, and preparing for a possible shot at goal after a back pass.

Goalkeeper Decathlon

The great majority of coaches, especially those of young soccer players, find it difficult to combine their training of the field players with a simultaneous coaching of goalkeepers. This is where knowing the 10 tests of the Goalkeeper Decathlon comes in handy. The coach may encourage the goalkeepers to practice on their own for short periods of time, assigning them one or two tests while coaching the rest of the team. This way, the goalkeepers occupy their time efficiently until the coach can again involve them in the training and learning processes of the entire team.

The decathlon can be used as a competition between any number of goalkeepers. If a club or a regional federation decides to organize a decathlon for a specific age group, setting aside two mornings or afternoons usually works well. Participation in this two-day competition (each of the days includes five tests against five different goalkeepers) generally motivates the contestants to improve in a great variety of abilities, such as positional play, techniques for saving shots, running out of goal, blocking shots while lying down, and different clearance techniques. A goalkeeper has the opportunity to analyze his or her level of playing and compare the performance with peers and opponents. In turn, the youngster may feel inspired or encouraged to improve by undertaking a series of corrective exercises for whatever deficiencies are observed in his or her skills.

The Goalkeeper Decathlon is also useful as a test to evaluate the level of performance among any number of goalkeepers. Not only can you evaluate the mastery of the specific goalkeepers' skills, but you can closely scrutinize other necessary aspects of an optimal performance: attention; anticipation; optical-motor perception; vision; correct, split-second decision making; will power and pluck; and physical capacities. Thanks to the Goalkeeper Decathlon, you have an ideal and fair selection of evaluation criteria.

Note: have goalkeepers between the ages of 10 and 13 years train using No. 4 balls and defending 7-on-7 soccer goals (with dimensions of 6 meters by 2 meters).

1. Penalty

Each goalkeeper starts with 3 points. The oldest one starts to defend the goal. If the attacking goalkeeper can't score from the penalty area of 9 meters, both switch positions and roles. When a goal is scored, the defending goalkeeper loses a point and continues to defend. The goalkeeper who reduces the opponent's score to zero is the winner.

TRAINING OBJECTIVES

- Mentally prepare to face the penalty kick with success.
- Concentrate only on the ball, without being influenced by other dummy movements of the attacker.
- Anticipate the ball's trajectory.
- Stretch out in a diagonal line—and not parallel to the goal line—to reduce the shooting angle.

2. Avoid the Dribbling of an Attacker

The attacking goalkeeper has four attacks (set out four balls) to dribble the ball from outside the penalty area into the goalkeeper's area. When he touches the ball, the defending goalkeeper comes out to prevent his penetrating with the ball into the small area. A goal can be scored only from inside the small area. An attack ends when the ball is out of the penalty area, a goal is scored, or the attacker commits an infringement. A penalty is awarded for an infringement of the defending goalkeeper. The winning goalkeeper is the player who concedes the fewest goals in four attacks.

TRAINING OBJECTIVES

- Learn to rush out of goal, cover the shooting angle, and get down to collect the ball from the attacker.
- Condition (or influence) the offensive play of the attacker by executing dummy movements.

- Be aggressive when necessary and act with determination.
- Select the precise moment for getting down, stretching out, and collecting the ball from the attacker.

3. Save Twice

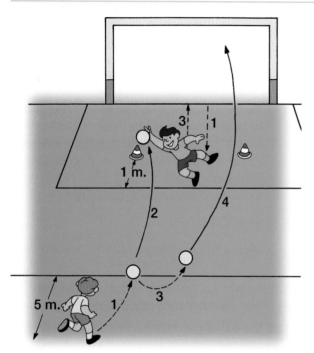

Use a 7-on-7 soccer field with a pair of cones marking an extra goal at 3.5 meters in front of the regular goal area. You can also use an 11-on-11 field, setting up the cones 4.5 meters in front of the goal line (see illustration). When the attacking goalkeeper starts 5 meters outside the penalty area, the defending goalkeeper rushes out of his goal to occupy the second one marked off by cones.

The attacking goalkeeper kicks her first ball from the edge of the area, allowing the defending one hardly time to reach the second goal line, assume an optimal, basic ready position, and make a save.

Immediately after the save (preferably managed in an upright position) or an inaccurate shot, a second stationary ball is kicked from 11 or 15 meters (compulsory), over the defender's head toward the official goal.

To be able to save the second shot directed to the official 7-on-7 goal, the goalkeeper runs backward and executes a second defensive action.

Each goalkeeper has three doublekicks from three different attacking positions.

The goalkeeper who concedes fewer goals is the winner.

TRAINING OBJECTIVES

- Improve coordination through running both forward and backward, making sudden stops, assuming simultaneously a correct, basic ready position and correct execution of different skills (catch, punch, deflection, save-clear, and dive), and even, when necessary, an acrobatic style.
- Develop power in the leg muscles.
- Demonstrate good positional play, always remaining on the imaginary line bisecting the shooting angle formed by the position of the ball and the two goalposts.
- Perfect the sense of direction and awareness.
- Quickly determine the most effective technique for avoiding the opponent's goals.

4. Two Touches

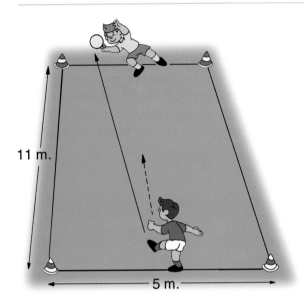

11 m.

5 m.

Set up a playing area 11 meters (can be 13 meters) long and 5 meters wide, fitting the size to your two goalkeepers' level of play. Each defends his or her own goal line. After the opening kick from one goal line, both goalkeepers may leave their respective goals to add pressure on the opponent. The response to the kick may have no more than two touches. In case of touching the ball more than twice in a row, a penalty is awarded the opponent and taken from the center of the field.

Duration of the game: two periods of 3 minutes.

TRAINING OBJECTIVES

- Kick the ball with either foot.
- Disguise the ball's trajectory.
- Improve optical-motor perception.
- Improve the ability to quickly assume a correct, basic ready position and appropriate positional play.
- Anticipate the opponent's play.
- As necessary, be able to modify one's own play (depending on the opponent's behavior).

5. Throw With One Hand

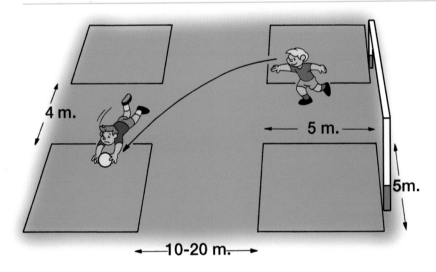

4 m.

5 m.

5m.

10-20 m.

Set up four squares measuring 5 meters per side, two in one zone and two in the opposite zone. A neutral zone, whose distance (10 to 20 meters) depends on the goalkeepers' level of power, separates the squares. Two goalkeepers face each other, taking a central position between their two squares. One throws the ball with the intention of having it land inside one of the two opponent's squares.

The defending goalkeeper, by intelligently reading and reacting, does whatever he or she can to move out of the initial central position and catch or clear the ball before its landing in either square. The winner is the goalkeeper who manages, with four throws only, to have the ball land inside one square of the opponent's zones the most.

TRAINING OBJECTIVES

- Improve throwing technique (as in discus throwing), accuracy, and power.
- Learn to disguise the direction of the throw.

6. Control of the Goalkeeper's Area

The attacking goalie disposes of six shots, executing two each from the sidelines of the 7-on-7 field and two more from the offside (13 meters) line but in front of the goal. The attacker's aim is to score a goal with either a free kick or getting the ball to touch the ground in the goalkeeper's area (4.5 by 12 meters) in front of the goal. In either case the defending goalkeeper would get a negative point. By using intelligent positional play, anticipation, and acrobatic moves, however, the defending goalkeeper tries to prevent the ball's entering the goal or landing in the small area. The goalkeeper who concedes fewer negative points is the winner.

TRAINING OBJECTIVES

- Develop the capacity to quickly make correct decisions after carefully observing the ball's trajectory and speed.
- Execute defensive actions (catch, dive, deflection, or punch) at maximum speed.
- Affect the attacker's shots by means of the positional play.
- Assume an optimal, basic ready position.
- Demonstrate will and nerve (even audacity).
- Improve optical-motor perception.
- Improve sense of direction and activity.

7. Stopping the Rebound

The younger of the two goalkeepers strikes a stationary ball from outside the penalty area to the goal, defended by the older player. This first goalie has four shots from four different attacking positions: two with a stationary ball and two with a moving one. Immediately after any powerful shot at goal, the attacker watches for a possible rebound, because the goalkeeper may *not block the ball* but instead may only intercept, deflect, deviate, or clear it.

When the first ball misses the goal, enters, or rebounds out of reach of the attacker, the attacking goalie runs to a second ball set down 6.5 meters away from the goal and 2 meters outside the small area. Both players fight for this second ball. While the goalkeeper tries to clear it from the penalty area, the attacker tries to score within less than 4 seconds after having executed the first shot.

If the attacker scores a goal with a direct shot with the first or second ball, the defending goalkeeper gets a negative point; for a goal obtained with a rebound, the goalie loses two points. The player who loses or concedes fewer goals after eight shots wins the match.

TRAINING OBJECTIVES

- Be prepared for a second defensive action after a first save!
- Improve perception and decision making.
- Improve coordination.

8. Accurate Clearances With Kicks

Mark off two goal squares, setting them not more than 10 meters apart from one another; their size will depend on the age of the goalkeepers. From some 20 to

25 m.

25 meters distance, the attacking goalkeeper kicks the ball (not too strongly) to the goal. Within 3 seconds, the defending goalkeeper collects the ball and clears it toward one of the two indicated squares on the right and left sides of his or her center midfield position. In the first two clearances the goalkeeper must use the drop kick and volley techniques. The objective is to get the ball to land in one of the two squares. In the third and fourth clearances the goalie uses a kick to simulate a restart of the game, with a stationary ball placed on the 4.5-meter line. The attacking goalkeeper tries everything possible to ensure that none of the clearances touches the ground in one of his or her two squares.

The goalkeeper who executes more correct clearances is the winner.

TRAINING OBJECTIVES

- Kick the ball with accuracy and power.
- Disguise the direction of the clearance.
- Vary the techniques used for the clearance.

9. Sprint to Clear the Ball First

Two goalkeepers play against each other. The coach or a neutral player bounces one ball from a distance of 9 meters in front of the goal. Both goalkeepers, starting from the same goal line, fight to clear the ball. The winning player is the one who manages to clear the ball out of the penalty area. This play is awarded one point.

The players continue with two more trials. For the second trial they start from a sitting position; for the third, they start from a prone (lying-down) position. The overall winner is the goalkeeper with the best result out of three clearances.

TRAINING OBJECTIVES

- Improve reaction time.
- Improve the ability to accelerate.
- Improve the ability to make good, quick decisions.
- Improve the ability to anticipate.
- Improve will power.

10. The Duel

The attacking goalkeeper starts with the ball at the edge of the penalty area. At this moment the defending goalkeeper may come out of the goal to stop the shot or dribble, always respecting the official rules of the game.

An attack ends when the ball leaves the penalty area, a goal is scored, the goalkeeper gains possession of the ball, the attacker commits an infringement, or the attack has lasted more than 4 seconds.

An infringement of the defending goalkeeper incurs a penalty.

The goalkeeper who concedes fewer goals in five attacks is the winner.

TRAINING OBJECTIVES

- Gain experience in positional play.
- Reduce the attacker's time and space by closing him or her down as quickly as possible.
- Force the attacker to do what the goalkeeper wants.
- Anticipate the technique of the shot at goal, as well as its trajectory.

The goalkeeper is considered the most important player on the team (any mistake this player makes could result in a goal against the team), and great importance and special attention should be given to his or her development. Because most goalkeeper errors are caused less by technique than by poor decision making, it's fundamental to train young goalkeepers not only in the technical but also the tactical aspects of play specific to the position. All young goalkeepers should be exposed regularly to a great variety of exercises and games in which they learn not only to save balls but also to consider both their opponents and teammates in their play.

PART IV

Coaching Players 12 Years and Up

The fourth level of the Soccer Development Model is designed for players ages 12 years and up. At this stage the coach can help forge a link from the children to the sport for the rest of their lives. This can only be accomplished, however, if the coach understands the players and exposes them to an effective and enjoyable soccer program that is tailored especially for them.

Soccer Players Between 12 and 14 Years

The intensive physical and hormonal transition induced by puberty leads to a loss of the children's balance in mobility and less response for the development of motor skills. It's therefore essential at this stage of the young players' evolution that they be exposed to collective or team activities in which they overcome their insecurity, unsteadiness, and also their sense of isolation, all characteristics of this age group.

By this time, youth become more socially aware, more inclined to "show off," and more prone to compete with their teammates and opponents for attention. They may also want to show their independence, and may even at this stage feel resentful of authority. For all these reasons, the older youth in this age group can already pose special problems to the coach, not only from the aspect of discipline but also in accepting what he or she teaches.

However, along with these problems, come a number of advantages. As the players are now much more responsive to cooperative activities with other players, this is an age group in which team play is learned with a certain ease. During this stage of their evolution, too, youth are used to making important decisions that may influence the formation or character of their personality.

If some of the team's players are genuine beginners and are unskilled, due to having started late in playing the game, this situation can pose a problem. They may lack the elementary ball-skill necessary for team play and not learn skills as easily or readily as they might have some years earlier.

Keeping all these characteristics in mind, here are some suggestions for coaching players between 12 and 14 years:

➤ Acknowledge the players' liking for competition by using competitive exercises, especially those that require the players to attain measurable objectives, such as passing the ball at a target.

➤ Consider every player as a singular individual.

➤ Encourage players as often as possible. Although this is important at all ages, and praise is always preferable to blame, 13 and 14 year olds are particularly sensitive to remarks of the coach that may reduce their status in the eyes of their friends. Therefore, avoid criticizing them in public!

➤ Since the players are physically bigger, and may have had experience in other sports, it may be necessary to be more clear-cut and stricter in applying the rules.

➤ The players are usually anxious to get into full-scale match play as often as possible. So you should explain to the players why each of the practice exercises is important for performing well in the match. This encourages them to accept the need for practice routines.

➤ Knowing "why" to do it and "what purpose" it serves is particularly important when it comes to motivating the young players to overcome, with a rich variety of physical stimuli, their lack of coordination, balance (equilibrium), mobility, or any deficiencies in speed, resistance, and strength. In fact, these stimuli for the development of physical capacities and coordination should be interwoven within the players' soccer sessions as often as possible.

A Different Coaching Style

Because the coach's philosophy and training program often decides whether a child at this age will stick with the game of soccer or look to other activities, coaches must strive to adapt to the sport's ever-changing demands. New knowledge appears daily, opening up possibilities we had never thought of some decades ago. What is considered valid today could already be out of date tomorrow, due to the frenetic evolution in many aspects of life.

The path to success in soccer is always under construction. The construction has to be seen as a process, not as an objective that must be reached in a particular given time. The game of soccer evolves continuously, and every coach should aim to adapt to its ever-changing demands to stay competitive.

One of the principle aims in the formation of soccer coaches is developing people who can do new things, without blindly repeating what other generations of coaches did in the past. Striving for excellence demands more creativity, innovation, and mental flexibility. Instead of teaching their players what they experienced during their career as player and coach, they must learn to unlock the innate and dormant potential of their players.

How can coaches achieve this? First of all, the tutors of future coaches (as well as those who already train players on a daily basis) should make sure that

➤ divergent thinking in their pupils is encouraged,

➤ every individual may freely express personal opinions,

➤ new technical-tactical movements are developed and applied,

➤ being creative and innovative is part of the success in the game, and

➤ players generate most of their knowledge and experience on their own.

To sum up, they should use a different teaching or coaching style—one based less on instructions or commands, with the pupils obeying and being pushed into a receptive or passive role. Instead of acting as a trainer or instructor, coaches should become consultants, observers, planners, or organizers of information and skills, trying to stimulate their pupils to advance and to excel until they are able to even surpass the coach's own limitations.

7

Games for 8-on-8 Soccer
Level 4

When intelligence, skill, and will work together, we can expect a masterpiece.

Having an integrated approach to learning, with practice in many simplified games and their variations or corrective activities, children are encouraged in the early levels of their development in soccer to continually interconnect their technical execution, tactical and overall knowledge, and other important capacities (vision, coordination, anticipation, determination, and physical qualities), all necessary elements for playing the game well.

This new model of development, unlike more traditional coaching, avoids the mistake of compartmentalizing the teaching of soccer in discrete disciplines (that is, techniques, tactics, physical fitness, *or* mental preparation). Instead, in this Soccer Development Model, children always experience and enjoy the game as a dynamic whole.

The step-by-step approach is one of the keys of success in this model, which uses the brain's innate ability to form memory-building connections. In the first three levels, all-important, basic game situations are broken down into series of small steps. These levels gradually and methodically lead to the final goal of youth soccer: to enjoy and successfully play the 8-on-8 game, an ideal bridge leading the young athletes within two years' practice to first playing the full soccer game.

Complete Soccer Test

We recommend that you use the Complete Soccer Test twice in the season, at its beginning and end, to get a comparison between the players' performance levels early and late in the season—and through this comparison a true result about their grade of improvement.

This is a simple test among different groups of six players. It assesses in a global context not only the players' technical, tactical, and physical capacities, but it also evaluates other essential aspects of the performance in soccer, such as effective perceiving, anticipating, understanding or communicating with teammates, decision making, and stress management.

Scoring for the Decathlon. The player who wins the most tests in the decathlon gets 6 points; the second best, 5; the third, 4; the fourth, 3; the fifth, 2; and the sixth, only 1 point.

Scoring for the 2-on-2 Triathlon Tests. For each of the three simplified games that a team wins, each player of that team gets 2 points.

Scoring for the 3-on-3 Triathlon Tests. For each of the three simplified games that a team wins, each player of that team gets 3 points.

Final Scoring. The player who wins the most points in the 16 tests is considered to be the all-around winning player of the six participants. If two players have the same score in the final classification, Event 10 of the decathlon serves as the tiebreaker.

The two players classified best of one group may challenge other winning players of two other groups, as may the third- and fourth-best or the fifth- and sixth- best. (The top two players of groups A, B, and C play a new tournament, as do the third- and fourth-ranked players of each group and the fifth- and sixth- ranked players.)

Simplified Games for 4 on 4

These games are a logical continuation of the simplified games in earlier chapters for fewer players. They build on the skills the young players have already learned, and in turn prepare them realistically for 8-on-8 soccer and, eventually, for the full game.

Assessing Players' Performance Levels

Order	Test	Confrontation between
1	2 on 2 with counterattack	Pair 1/6 on 2/5, 3/4 on 1/6, 2/5 on 3/4
2	1st test of the decathlon	1 on 6, 2 on 5, 3 on 4
3	2nd test of the decathlon	1 on 5, 2 on 4, 3 on 6
4	2 on 2 with 4 intersecting goals	Pair 1/4 on 2/6, 3/5 on 1/4, 2/6 on 3/5
5	3rd test of the decathlon	1 on 4, 2 on 3, 5 on 6
6	4th test of the decathlon	1 on 3, 2 on 6, 4 on 5
7	2 on 2 with two wide goals	Pair 1/5 on 2/6, 3/4 on 2/6, 1/5 on 3/4
8	5th test of the decathlon	1 on 2, 3 on 5, 4 on 6
9	6th test of the decathlon	1 on 6, 2 on 5, 3 on 4
10	3 on 3 with 4 intersecting goals	Team 1/2/3 vs. 4/5/6
11	7th test of the decathlon	1 on 5, 2 on 4, 3 on 6
12	8th test of the decathlon	1 on 4, 2 on 3, 5 on 6
13	3 on 3 with counterattack	Team 1/2/4 vs. 3/5/6
14	9th test of the decathlon	1 on 3, 2 on 6, 4 on 5
15	10th test of the decathlon	1 on 2, 3 on 5, 4 on 6
16	3 on 3 with two wide goals	Team 1/3/6 vs. 2/4/5

1st Simplified Game
4 on 2 in Adjacent Squares

Set up the two 15-meter squares, as in the illustration, and form two teams of four players each. The team with the youngest players places its four players in one area, but the second team distributes its players between both areas: two in the first and two in the adjacent square. The four players of the first team try to pass the ball as often as possible among their team. Their objective is also to prevent the ball's running across the sides of the square or losing it to the two defenders, who are trying meanwhile to gain possession of the ball. If the second team's members do get possession, the defenders must pass the ball quickly to their teammates in the neighboring field. Immediately after the pass, they join their teammates in the adjacent square, followed by two former attackers who now defend in that new area. To be able to play a pressing defense against the four attackers, it is advisable that after every change of possession of the ball, the two freshest or closest defenders run quickly into the other area.

When the ball played by any of the four attackers leaves the playing area, a kick-in is awarded to the two defenders to one of their teammates in the adjacent square, with the defender at a distance of at least 5 meters. To help motivate the players, call out every pass loudly. Each team tries to complete first 15, and later 21 passes, to win the first set. The winning team is the one that attains the established number of passes in two sets.

VARIATIONS

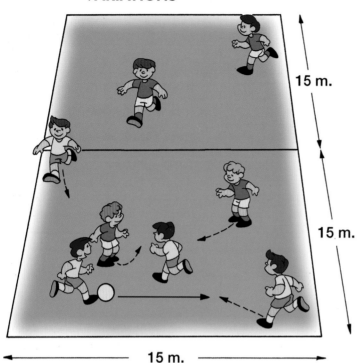

15 m.

15 m.

15 m.

➤ Count only those passes that cover more than 5 meters.

➤ The attackers try to keep the ball in their possession for 15 (later for 20) seconds (also see the Ninth Simplified Game "Maintaining Ball Possession 2 on 1" in chapter 4).

➤ After a successful pass is executed, the player must immediately run at least 5 meters in any direction.

➤ Three teams of four players participate. In one square, the four teammates of Team 1 play against two of the players from Team 2. In the adjacent square, the other two teammates from Team 2 defend against the four players of Team 3. The team of four players which can keep possession the longest wins.

TRAINING OBJECTIVES

- Maintain a high level of concentration for at least two sets.
- Avoid a 1-on-1 situation, instead looking out systematically for the "2-on-1."
- Avoid entering into the range of action of any defender when you have the ball, and try to pass it as soon as you have committed the defender. Use direct or wall passes as often as possible.
- As an attacker, learn to time dummies precisely to gain space, time, and self-confidence, especially when you are drawn into a corner of the field where fewer passing options exist.
- Learn to run away from the defenders and make yourself available for a pass in a zone that is not controlled by the defense and that is not too close to the ball carrier. Receiving the ball in a position far away from the defense allows you more time and space to control it and play it again.
- Make yourself available in a zone not already occupied by a teammate.
- Pass the ball with speed and accuracy.
- Avoid indicating the direction of the intended pass to your opponents.
- Bend your legs and keep your center of gravity as low as possible to the ground when defending.
- Invite the ball carrier, through a body movement, to play the ball in the direction you want him or her to pass.
- Be aggressive when you defend, prepared to go full-out to reduce the time and space at the disposal of the attackers.
- Consider the position of your defender teammates before you go for the ball. The defense is generally more effective against attackers situated in a corner of the field.

CORRECTIVE GAMES

Four players place themselves around an 8-meter square without being allowed to enter it. They should pass the ball to each other in such a way that it always runs along the ground and crosses two sides of the square before being received and controlled. Two defenders inside the square try their best to prevent the four external players from executing the passes during 2 minutes of play. After 2 minutes, the two defenders switch roles and positions with two of the attackers. The game is over when every player has defended for 2 minutes.

VARIATIONS

➤ Only first-time passes (no control of the ball is allowed before it is passed) across two of the lines count.

➤ A fifth attacker is introduced, positioned inside the square to receive a pass from one of the four teammate players outside the square. They may choose between a pass across two lines to another external player (to score 1 point) or to the fifth player inside the square. Every control of the ball by the fifth player with a subsequent pass to a teammate outside the square counts 3 points.

2nd

Simplified Game
Fast Attack 4 on 2 With Three Teams

The game is played with three teams, each having four players, on a 7-on-7 or 8-on-8 soccer field. To start play, give a visible signal to two of the teams, both on the centerline and in possession of a ball. They attack their respective goals in opposite directions. Two players of the third team defend each of these goals (see illustration). The team that manages to score first wins. When the two defenders and neutral goalkeeper gain possession, they must clear the ball across the centerline. After five attacks and a complete rest in between them, the three teams rotate until each team has defended 5 times and attacked 10 times.

VARIATIONS

➤ Once the attackers have started their offensive moves, the defenders leave their positions—on the penalty area line, 10 meters behind any sideline, or even on the same centerline—in order to pursue and stop them from scoring.

➤ The attack begins from a limited area (15 by 15 meters marked close to the centerline, sideline, or both), positioned in the left or right wing.

TRAINING OBJECTIVES

- Attack in a diamond formation, that is, with depth and width.
- Use long, direct passes in preference to horizontal passes.
- Try as often as possible to make a first-time play.
- Gain experience in goal scoring.
- As defenders, learn to delay and channel the attack.

CORRECTIVE GAMES

Consult the dribbling games, the simplified games for 2 on 2 (chapter 4), and the Second Simplified Game for 3 on 3 (chapter 5) for some good choices of remedial games.

3rd

Through Passes to a "Shadowed" Forward

Review the rules for the Eighth Simplified Game in chapter 5. This game is played on a 7-on-7 soccer field by two teams. Each team has two midfield players (who play between the two penalty areas), one forward (always situated in the opposing penalty area), and a fourth player who defends while remaining in the narrow zone formed by the offside line (at 13 meters) and the proper penalty area (at 11 meters). If there are no offside lines, the defender should move only on the 11-meter line. The two midfield players in possession of the ball try to pass to their forward, sending the ball into the opposing penalty area once the forward becomes available for a through pass. After controlling the ball (in an *offside position*), the outlet player attempts to score against a neutral goalkeeper. The defender in the zone between the 11-meter and 13-meter lines tries to cover the zone, defending against any potential pass to this "outlet" player behind him. None of the players may leave his or her assigned zone. Every 5 minutes the midfield players of each team change positions and functions with their team's forward and defender.

VARIATIONS

➤ Once the ball has entered the shooting zone, any midfield player or the defender may run into the penalty area to support the "outlet" player or to defend. Any attacker may score now.

➤ To learn the attack from the second line, participants apply the rule that only one of the midfield players may score after having served the ball to the front runner.

➤ Advanced players should practice the through pass to a forward, who is closely marked by a defender inside the penalty area. Also have the players review the Seventh and Eighth Simplified Games for teams of two players (chapter 4) to improve their ability at playing through passes and to work on the reception and control of the ball while being marked. This game variation works well on a mini-soccer field.

TRAINING OBJECTIVES

In attack these are the objectives:

- Maintain a high level of concentration during two periods of 5 minutes.
- Show strong communication and cooperation skills. The player who wishes to receive the ball should establish a visual agreement with the ball carrier, always signaling him or her where to pass the ball.
- Look up while dribbling the ball; after having analyzed the situation, using knowledge of the soccer game, select the most efficient pass.
- Give preference to a through pass over a square pass or dribble.
- Determine what to do next before receiving the ball to be able to continue the play as fluently as possible.
- Switch quickly from attack to defense when the ball is lost.
- Once the forward receives the through pass, his reception technique should consider the next move and the presence of a defender (see the last variation) to be able to score in less time.

In defense these are the objectives:

- Quickly switch from defense to attack when the ball is won.
- Make the through pass difficult for the attackers by systematically reducing their space and time.
- Cooperate in defense, always considering the positions of defensive teammates before executing a tackle.
- Read the play of the attackers to anticipate their intentions in time.

CORRECTIVE GAMES

Use the Eighth Simplified Game for 3 on 3 (see chapter 5).

4th Simplified Game
Rescue of Prisoners

Mark off a square playing area that is 25 meters on each side, using a cone goal in each corner. Two players of one team compete against two players of the other team in this area. The teams' third and fourth players stand in diagonally opposite corners of the playing area (see illustration). The aim of the two attackers is to play 10 consecutive passes without letting the ball go out of the area's limits. The ball carrier may pass the ball to his teammate who tries to receive in the center of the square or to one of his two teammates ("prisoners") in the diagonally opposed corners ("prisons"). When the prisoner receives the ball at his respective prison goal, he is released from standing stationary, moves out of the "prison," and dribbles or passes the ball to any other teammate. The former passer then assumes the position in "prison."

Meanwhile, the two defenders in the center do their best to prevent the team in possession of the ball from successfully passing. Every pass should be counted loudly enough to inform both the coach and opponents about the actual standing of the game. When the ball leaves the assigned playing area, a kick-in is awarded, with the defenders at a distance of at least 3 meters. The team that manages to play 10 consecutive passes three times or that keeps the ball in its possession longer is considered the winner.

VARIATIONS

Use these variations of the game in the following order of progress:

1. Only long passes (more than 10 meters or from one part of the field to the other) count; draw a centerline to split the square in two areas.

2. Only passes without a previous dribble count.

3. A player can be released from "prison" only when the pass to him is precise (that is, through the goal cones in his corner).

4. Instead of remaining in the small "prisons," each of the four receivers chooses a position just behind one of the square's four sidelines from which to receive a pass from teammates.

5. Only one receiver has to stay outside the square, being available to receive a pass anywhere outside the field (that is, 3 on 3 plus one outside player).

6. All four prisoners must constantly run, using different speeds and going in any direction around the playing field to be a positions for receiving the pass.

7. For improving first-time play, only first-time passes count.

8. To improve receiving and control of the ball, the prisoners are released only after an aerial pass.

9. To improve head-kick techniques, the prisoner may change positions with the passer only if she manages to play the ball with a head-kick.

10. Practice these variations with 5, 6, 7, and then 8 players on each team; increase the dimensions of the playing area as the numbers of players increases.

TRAINING OBJECTIVES

- Be aware of all options before passing the ball to be able to select the most effective move (this is usually a pass to the player furthest away from the defenders).

- Make it simple and look for a high percentage of success in your passes; avoid getting into a 1-on-1 situation and keep the ball out of the range of action of any defender.

- Develop accuracy and speed with any pass, also trying to disguise its direction.

- Also see the objectives of the First Simplified Game in this chapter.

5th Simplified Game
Executing Consecutive Passes

30 m.

30 m.

Two teams of four players compete between the center-line and the offside line of a 7-on-7 soccer field (or in a square with 30-meter sides on an 8-on-8 soccer field), trying to keep possession of the ball and execute 10 consecutive passes from a distance of at least 10 meters. The official soccer rules apply. After one team manages to pass the ball 10 times in succession, there should be a 2-minute rest interval before the game resumes. During the interval the players of both teams evaluate their performance level. The game is restarted with a ball toss. To win the game it's necessary to complete 10 consecutive passes three times.

VARIATIONS

➤ The team that keeps the ball in its possession longer is the winner.

➤ Play the game in a smaller area (a square of 20-meter sides).

➤ Two players from each team stay on a side of the square (that is, there is one player on each side of the square) without being allowed to enter it. For the midfield players to improve their perception and attention, the "outlet" players should avoid standing still on any line.

TRAINING OBJECTIVES

- Avoid a concentration of players close to the ball in order to make the defense more difficult.
- Read the game correctly to be able to select the most effective passing option.
- Learn to keep possession of the ball in critical situations, such as when opponents apply a pressing defense or when the ball carrier is drawn into a corner of the field.
- Know when to pass and when not to pass (to dribble instead).
- Learn to shield the ball with the body.
- Add width and depth to the attack in order to stretch the opponent's defense; the attackers without the ball should constantly be ready to receive in those zones of the playing area less under the control of the defenders.
- Before the execution of any pass, ensure that some visual agreement occurs between ball carrier and receiver.
- Play as a team and reduce individual play (especially 1 on 1) as much as possible.
- As defenders, place more players close to the ball than the attackers do; read the game to anticipate the next moves from the attacking side and to condition the opponent's play.

6th Simplified Game
Dribbling Across the Opponents' End Line

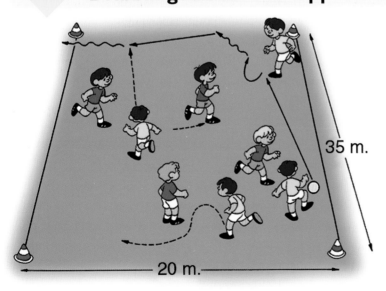

35 m.

20 m.

Use a 7-on-7 soccer field or an area 20 meters by 35 meters. Two teams of four players each compete between the centerline and the offside line, aiming to dribble the ball across the opposing end line (that is, 35 meters away). The game starts with a toss of ball. All free kicks must be taken at a spot at least 4.5 meters away from the respective end line. There is no offside. All other rules are the same as the official ones.

Duration of the game: three periods of 3 minutes each, with intervals of 2 minutes in which both teams should rest and elaborate the tactics for the next 3 minutes of play.

VARIATIONS

➤ Before competing in this game, youngsters should practice the following variation of it: each team has five attacks, starting always from their proper end line. When they touch the ball for the first time, their opponents initiate the defense from the opposite end line. The attack finishes with either a goal or a loss of the possession of the ball to the defenders. The defenders may not counterattack after having defended with success, however. The team that scores more goals in 10 attacks is the winner.

➤ More advanced players should practice in a smaller playing area (easier to defend) or in a much bigger area (to make the defense very difficult).

➤ This variant could be called "Make It and Take It." After scoring, the attackers *continue* to attack. They immediately turn around to attack the opposite goal, which should be defended by the same opponents. The team that manages to score more goals in 5 minutes of play is the winner.

➤ Instead of attacking two wide goal areas, the attackers now try to score in either of two 6-meter-wide goals situated in the wing positions on the two end lines.

➤ Each team is in possession of one ball. To score the team must control one ball on the opposing end line and also be in possession of the other one.

TRAINING OBJECTIVES

In attacking these are the objectives:

- Play with a "rhombus formation" and ensure width and depth in the attack.
- Lift the head while dribbling the ball to collect information that will allow you to pass the ball to the best-situated teammate.
- Know when to change the rhythm of the attack; learn to accelerate at the correct moment.
- Learn to be available as receiver in a part of the playing area that is not controlled by the defenders; this zone is usually farther away from the ball, at the opposite side of the field from where the ball is.
- Select the most effective passing option; don't risk long passes when the likelihood of success is poor.
- Know what the correct option is for beating a pressing defense.
- Know how to execute free kicks and the kick-in successfully.
- Avoid getting into a 1-on-1 situation, which has little likelihood of success; instead aim to create 2-on-1 situations through systematic support of the ball carrier.

In defending these are the objectives:

- Position yourself between the opponent and the proper goal, staying closer to the center of the field than is the opponent.
- Scan the game situation, observing in particular the ball but remembering to keep both the opponents and your teammates in your field of vision.
- Ensure width and depth in your defense.
- Anticipate the ball carrier's intentions.

- Follow the game situation and practice a combined marking (marking closely in your assigned zone), a zonal marking, or a player-to-player marking with constant communication among all four defenders.
- Use a side position to tackle an attacker in full control of the ball.
- Maintain a high level of concentration during the game.

CORRECTIVE GAMES

Many game situations that occur frequently in this game will help players improve their skill levels. Any of the simplified games for teams of two (see chapter 4) or three (see chapter 5) are good.

Simplified Game

7th Long Passes out of the Midfield

Two teams of four players only compete between the centerline and the offside line of a 7-on-7 soccer field. The game lasts for three periods of 5 minutes each. Start with a ball toss in the center of the field. Each team then tries to gain possession of the ball and pass it, pressured by the defense of the opponents, through one of the two goal areas (marked by cones set 3 meters apart) established some 13 meters behind the opponent's end line. No player may leave the assigned playing area. It helps the flow of play to place some reserve balls on each end line in order to restart the game without delay after any long pass. While the attacking team does its best to create sufficient space and gain some time to prepare a long, precise pass, the opponents defend aggressively. Defenders try to always outnumber the attackers in the zone where the ball is being played. The young players will quickly learn that immediately after a successful tackle, there is an ideal opportunity to counterattack with a long pass.

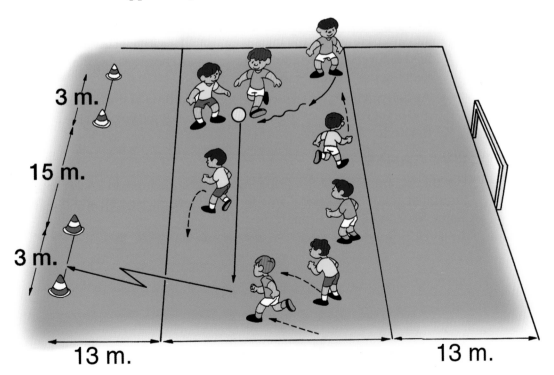

3 m.

15 m.

3 m.

13 m.   13 m.

VARIATIONS

Have players try the variations in the progressive order listed here:

1. A neutral player supports whatever team is in possession of the ball.

2. At least three passes should be played in the center of the field before a long pass can be executed.

3. A fifth attacker waits behind the two goal areas to receive the through pass and then finish the attack with a shot into the 7-on-7 goal.

4. Instead of introducing an attacker as in the previous variation, a defender now stays close to each of the goals, trying to intercept the long pass to either of the goals.

5. Play the same game (variation 4) on a smaller field.

6. Two attackers, watched by one defender between them, are prepared to receive behind each of the goals. Their aim is to collect a long pass out of the midfield through one of the two pairs of cones, despite the defender's efforts to the contrary.

7. Remove the goals (cones) but station the two attackers more or less at the same place, about 13 meters behind the end line. After receiving the long through pass, the attackers must score, despite the active presence of one defender and a goalkeeper.

8. Play as in Variation 8, but include a second defender who marks closely.

9. Play as in Variation 9, but add a third defender who acts as a free player.

TRAINING OBJECTIVES

- Fulfill the coaching objectives of the previous simplified games.
- Aim to execute a long pass immediately after the recovery of the ball from the opponent.
- Learn to disguise the direction of the pass.
- Analyze the game situation before receiving the ball to find out whether a long pass is possible.
- Always look out for the long pass, but when its execution doesn't seem likely to lead to success, forget about it and instead choose a play that ensures your team's keeping possession of the ball.
- As defenders, try to reduce the space and time at the disposal of the ball carrier and his or her supporting players; after having recovered the ball, switch quickly to attack.

CORRECTIVE GAMES

Use the Second, Fifth, or Seventh Simplified Game for 2 on 2 (see chapter 4); the Fifth, Eighth, or Tenth Simplified Game for 3 on 3 (see chapter 5); and the Third Simplified Game for 4 on 4 (in this chapter).

8th

Simplified Game

Score, Defend, and Counterattack

Form two teams of four players each who will compete in half of the 7-on-7 or 8-on-8 soccer field. Use an official goal of 6 by 2 meters and add two 6-meter-wide goals marked by cones on the centerline. It's also a good idea to add one neutral goalkeeper on each team. Start the game with a ball toss in the center of the field. Both teams toss a coin to decide which will first attack the official goal and which will instead try to score by a pass from any distance through one of the two goals on the centerline. For any infringement of the rules consult the 7-on-7 or 8-on-8 game rules, depending on the ages of the players.

Duration of the game: four periods of 5 minutes each; at each interval the teams change sides and goals.

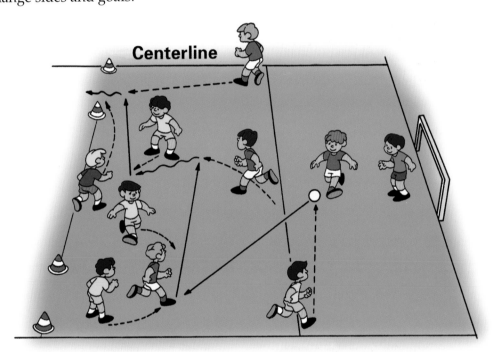

Centerline

TRAINING OBJECTIVES

- Strive for the objectives of the previous simplified games for four-player teams.
- Know how to play effectively in the opposing shooting area.
- Watch systematically for the goalkeeper's rebound.
- Know how to execute free kicks well; gain experience in building up the defensive wall.
- Gain experience in the corners and the penalty area.
- Know how to defend without giving away a penalty.

CORRECTIVE GAMES

Review any of the previous simplified games as well as the "Games for Basic Abilities and Capacities" (chapter 3).

9th

Simplified Game

Shooting Game With Four Goals

Form three teams that will use half of an 8-on-8 soccer field. Ten meters inside the side or end lines of the half, you should add four goal areas with cones (6 meters wide). One team's four players defend the four open goals that you set out with cones. The other two teams attack or defend depending on which team has the ball. Their aim is to score in either goal from inside the playing area. After each goal the goalkeeper clears the ball high into the air. The game continues when the ball runs behind any of the goals, but when it moves out of the marked area, one of several reserve balls close to each goal area should be brought into play by the goalkeeper of that goal. After every 5 minutes, the teams rotate so that the goals are defended by a different team. The team that scores the most goals in 15 minutes of play is the winner.

A fourth team could take part with the role of collecting the balls shot out of the field and replacing them close to the nearest goal area.

VARIATION

➤ Only shots from a distance of more than 8 meters or kicks executed with the less-skillful foot count as a goal.

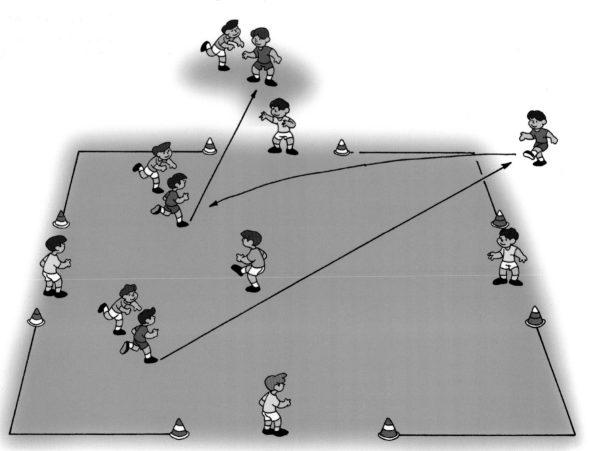

10th Simplified Game
Shooting Game With Three Goals

Form two teams of four players each to take part, and have them use a No. 4 soccer ball. Neither team may step into the center circle of the full field in which three goals are situated in a triangular formation at distances of 6 meters (see the illustration). The teams' aim is to score in any of these three goals, which are defended by a neutral goalie who runs quickly from one goal line to the other (depending on where the ball is being played at the moment). After a goal is scored, the game continues without any stop; if the goalkeeper interferes successfully, she or he clears the ball into the air. To avoid any concentration of players around the ball, the coach may allow only two players of each team to play in one half of the soccer field.

TRAINING OBJECTIVES

- Improve the goalkeeper's positional play.
- Score despite the presence of a defender.
- Consider the position of teammates before attempting to score.

CORRECTIVE GAMES

Choose from games in Level 1's, "Passing, Receiving, and Shooting Games" and from chapter 6, "Developing Young Goalkeepers."

11th Simplified Game
Mixed Soccer With Head Kicks

Play across the width of a 7-on-7 soccer field on two goals. Each team plays soccer in its own half, but changes to "handball" after managing to pass the ball into the hands of a teammate who receives it beyond the centerline. When playing handball in the opponent's half of the field, the main objective is to pass precisely with the hands to a teammate who is close to the opposing goal, helping him to score with a head kick. The defenders must defend as soccer players. Initially no goalkeepers are used, but as the players progress in this game, you may introduce one in each goal. Do not allow the goalie at first to rush out from the goal line.

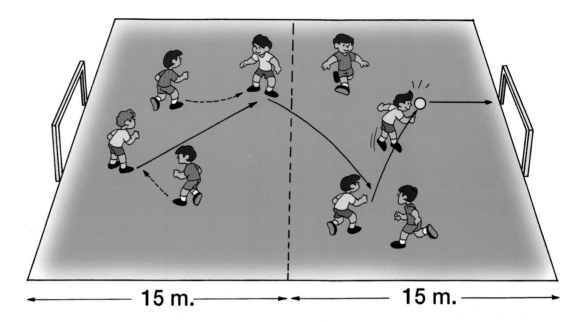

← —— **15 m.** —— → ← —— **15 m.** —— →

VARIATION

➤ Play the game without restrictions for the goalkeepers. The attackers may also score with a kick from their own half of the field.

TRAINING OBJECTIVES

- Gain experience in scoring with a head kick.
- Develop the capacity to adapt quickly to new problems or game situations.
- Improve the game without the ball.

CORRECTIVE GAMES

Traditional exercises for introducing, consolidating, and perfecting the technical aspects of the head kick in a sitting, kneeing, and standing position are all useful here.

12th Simplified Game
4 on 2 With Head Kicks

Use the rules of the Eleventh Simplified Game for 3 on 3 (see chapter 5) with two exceptions: the game is played by teams of four players and only one ball is used for both teams. Two players on each team start as wings, and two start in the center of the field. The team that gains possession of the ball after the initial ball throw then passes the ball to one of its two wings, who is marked by the opposing wing. Once a wing manages to control the ball within his limited zone with three consecutive touches, he may advance without opposition. After he arrives level with the penalty area, he centers the ball to one of his two teammates in the central zone. These teammates should be supporting him during his dribbling, with the aim to then score with a head kick. They are opposed, however, by two defenders playing in the center stripe. Initially there are no goalkeepers, which makes scoring with a head kick easier. After ten attacks, the four players of each team rotate, until everybody has played in the three possible positions.

VARIATIONS

Have players practice these variations in the order of progression given here:

1. The game is first played without defenders. Both teams attack, every one in possession of one ball (as described in the Eleventh Simplified Game for 3 on 3 in chapter 5).

2. When the attackers manage to score frequently with a head kick, the game is made more complex and is played with one ball only. One of the two center players of the opposing team is allowed to defend as a field player, while the other one remains on the centerline.

3. Follow Variation 2, except that the only defender has to play as goalkeeper; the goalie can defend only with both feet on the goal line.

4. There are no limitations for the two opposing defenders in the center stripe, once they realize that their team is not going to attack. In general, one of them runs quickly into the goal to serve as goalkeeper, while the second one tries to intercept the center.

5. Play the rules of the original game (described above).

6. Play the original game with two neutral goalkeepers (see illustration).

7. The wings may choose between a center and a shot toward the goal, which is defended by a goalkeeper.

8. The wing who is not in possession of the ball may join his two attackers in the center stripe and participate in the goal scoring (making it 3 on 2).

9. Play as a free game except that a goal may be scored only with a head kick.

TRAINING OBJECTIVES

Use the same objectives as for the Eleventh Simplified Game for 3 on 3 (chapter 5).

CORRECTIVE GAMES

Use the Eleventh Simplified Game for 3 on 3 (chapter 5).

Simplified Games for 5 on 5

Review the first eight simplified games for 4 on 4. All these games should be practiced with the same rules (including the same field dimensions and durations of the matches); simply add one more player on each team.

The training objectives and corrective exercises also remain the same for these more difficult and complex games as the ones given in the earlier simplified games for playing 4 on 4.

Level 4 Competitions

Three or four times during a season you can replace a training session with the 5-on-5 Triathlon to give the 12- and 13-year-old players an opportunity to compete, under more stressful conditions, in the most common situations of the 8-on-8 soccer game.

5-on-5 Triathlon

Hold a competition among teams of five players each. Use the score sheet in the illustration on page 203, which again gives examples of teams named after European countries.

1. Dribble Across the Opponents' End Line

The first game is played between the two offside lines of the 7-on-7 soccer field (see illustration for placement of cones). Both teams try to control the ball on the opponent's offside line. A ball throw starts the game. Free kicks and throw-ins should always be more than 4.5 meters away from the offside line.

Duration of the game: three periods of 3 minutes.

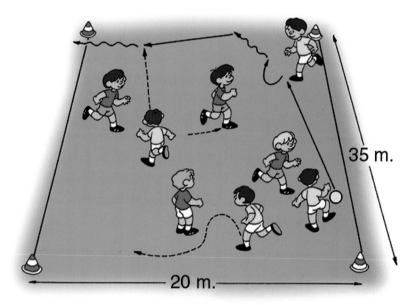

Europe against South America

Teams	Colombia	Bolivia	Peru
Names of players			

Teams	France	Poland	Holland
Names of players			

First game: Dribble across the opponent's end line (3 × 3 min.)

Scores:

BOL-FRA		
COL-POL		
PER-HOL		

Second game: Long passes out of the midfield (3 × 3 min.)

Scores:

BOL-POL		
COL-HOL		
PER-FRA		

Third game: Score, defend, and counterattack (4 × 3 min.)

Scores:

BOL-HOL		
COL-FRA		
PER-POL		

Final result: Europe against South America _____ _____
(sum of victories)

Duration of the triathlon tournament: 2 hours and 15 minutes

Technical delegate: _____

Note: During the triathlon, changing the composition of the team is not permitted.

Organization of the 5-on-5 triathlon.

2. Long Passes out of the Midfield

Add cones to mark off two goal areas (about 3 meters wide) across from and to either side of the field's regular goal (see illustration for the other dimensions). From a position in between the two offside lines, each team tries to pass the ball through one of the two extra goal areas. To save time, you should have several reserve balls available.

Duration of the game: three periods of 3 minutes.

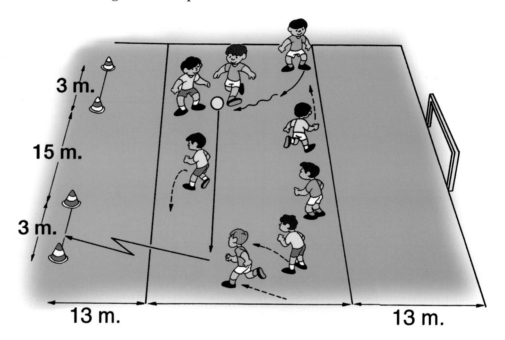

3 m.

15 m.

3 m.

13 m.   13 m.

3. Score, Defend, and Counterattack

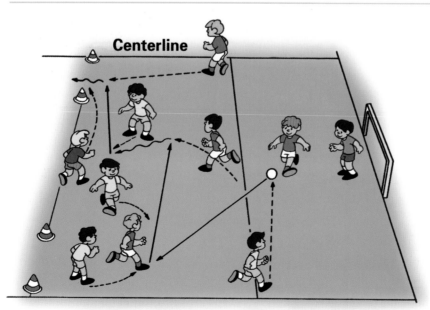

Centerline

Use half of a 8-on-8 soccer field, again adding cones to set up two goal areas across from the regular, 6-meter-wide goal and just off the centerline (see illustration). It's a good idea to use a neutral goalkeeper in the regular goal. Start with a ball toss in the center of the field. One team attacks the regular goal. The other defends it and counterattacks with a pass through one of the two added goal areas.

Duration of the game: four periods of 3 minutes; after each 3 minutes, the teams switch positions and functions.

8-on-8 Soccer

The 8-on-8 soccer game is a solid bridge that leads the 12- and 13-year-old players from the popular 7-on-7 game toward the full game.

Rules of the Game

The following rules apply only to 8-on-8 soccer. For any circumstance not covered in the following regulations, consult the official rules of the game of soccer.

Playing Field

The 8-on-8 soccer game is played between the penalty areas of the official soccer field (see illustration). The penalty areas are the zones between the 16.5-meter line of the official field (the end line of the 8-on-8 field) and the centerline. Mobile goals from the 7-on-7 game are used and put in the center of the 16.5-meter line of the official field. The penalty spot is situated at a distance of 9 meters from the goal "mouth."

Size of the Ball

Continue to use a No. 4 soccer ball for all competitions!

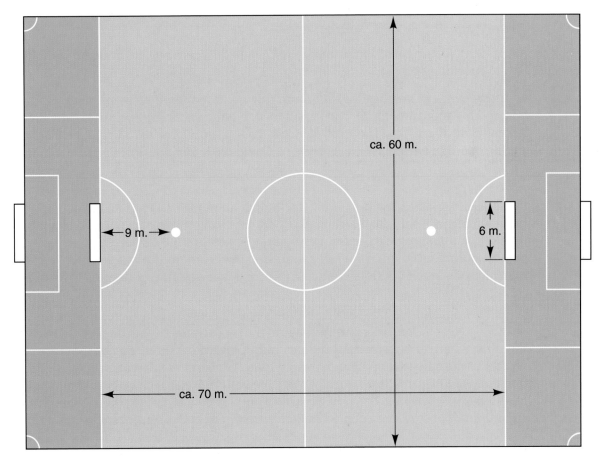

The 8-on-8 playing field. This competition is played between the penalty areas of the official soccer field.

Number of Players

A team has a maximum of 11 players. Eight of them at a time are involved in the game. A substituted player may return at any time and as often as the coach decides. All 11 players must participate in the competition.

Duration

The competition last three periods of 25 minutes each, with 5 minutes rest between them.

Free Kicks and Penalties

For any infringement of a defender in his own half, the referee awards, depending on the severity, a free kick or a penalty (from 9 meters); in addition, the referee may card the player, adding a yellow card (temporary suspension up to 10 minutes) or a red card (ejection from the game).

Referee

To promote young players' learning to umpire, the 8-on-8 soccer competition should be controlled by a referee (without assistants) under 20 years of age.

Advantages of 8-on-8 Soccer

The 8-on-8 soccer game better matches 12- and 13-year-old players than the official 11-on-11 competition in several areas:

1. Each player touches the ball more often and is therefore more involved in the game. This more intensive participation not only enhances technical and tactical learning but also allows the youth coach to collect more precise information about the performance of each player as well as of his whole team as a unit.

2. Although the parameters of space and time are almost exactly the same (290 square meters per player or 300 square meters per player) as in the 11-on-11 game, the 8-on-8 game assures better learning (and facilitates a smooth transition to regular play) because there are only 16 players in the field. With fewer players on the field, the basic game situations appear more frequently, but they confront the young players with less complex problems than in the full game. The players therefore can feel more capable, which results in self-confidence and, at the same time, greater motivation to learn even more.

3. Playing with the No. 4 ball size allows youngsters to reach any player on the field with a pass (something that is impossible to find with their playing on the full field with the official ball). This aspect stimulates their perception skills. Besides, the size and weight of the ball are in perfect harmony with the level of speed and power of these players (especially true for the girls). With the ball tailored to their physical and mental capacities, better results occur in the acquiring and consolidating the most important techniques. This can't happen when youth compete in the traditional game with the official ball, therefore having fewer chances at the ball because of the excessive numbers of players on each team.

The 8-on-8 competition therefore helps young players to develop correct habits for later use in the 11-on-11 game. There is no question that it's much easier to integrate a player successfully into the full game after she or he has been exposed to two years of simpler problems in the 8-on-8 game.

"Training is a process of development through gradually increasing demands."

L. Morehouse

4. All young goalkeepers between 12 and 14 years prefer to play 8-on-8 soccer instead of the full game. Why? Like their teammates they, too, have the opportunity to play the ball more often because fewer players are involved in the game and because the ball approaches the vicinity of the goals more often. Therefore, they gain more experience in less time. And the size of the goal is perfectly tailored to their height.

5. With the ball more often played close to the goal, the forwards and defenders also gain valuable experiences in the most decisive parts of the field—where any mistake or successful action can modify the result of the game. In 8-on-8 soccer they learn to deal with stressful situations and to take offensive and defensive rebounds.

6. With only eight players on a team, the game has fewer interruptions with the ball in play more time.

7. There is no physical overloading of any player because the coach may change a player as frequently and as often as he considers wise. "Rolling substitution" improves the team spirit and at the same time develops more versatile players who are capable of playing well in different positions. Due to the shorter distances in 8 on 8, there are less stimuli for anaerobic resistance, which at this stage of the development of the player has to be considered positive. Despite the poor level of explosive power, the

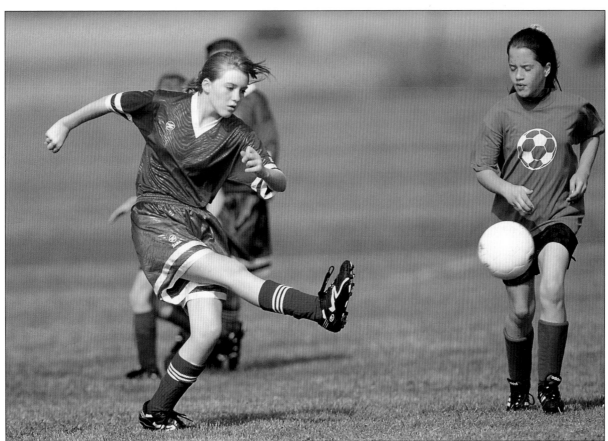

The **8-on-8** competition successfully prepares players for the official 11-on-11 game.

© Joe Robbins

No. 4 ball can be passed to any player in any part of the field, thus stimulating development of the perceptive capacities.

8. The job of the youth coach, who generally is not very experienced, is much easier. He or she learns under simpler conditions (fewer players but more ball contacts, less complex game situations) to analyze the players' performance and the team as a whole, as well as how to facilitate programming the contents for the next training sessions. The greater facility in analysis makes it easier to find appropriate solutions to problems.

9. What is valid for the coach is valid also for the referee. Putting a logical progression of youth competitions into practice will also, without doubt, benefit the level of umpiring in the long term. Like the coach and his or her young players, young referees also grow slowly—by facing increasingly difficult and complex problems—into the full game, ensuring that they feel capable at each stage of their referee development.

10. Spectators, especially parents, really enjoy watching an 8-on-8 game more than the traditional one because it's easier to follow. Because there are more goal opportunities for both teams, it's more exciting. Moreover, because of the larger penalty areas between the centerlines and the 16.5-meter line of the full field (almost 40 meters deep and 55 meters wide), fair play must be practiced to not give away penalties to the opponents. That is why far fewer injuries occur when the rules of 8-on-8 soccer are applied. Last but not least, the parents see their daughters and sons in possession of the ball more frequently; they see more successful interventions than in the full game—and more possibilities of scoring.

A solid bridge between learning more complex situations and applying them in a competitive game is presented in this chapter. Here a great variety of simplified games and their corrective exercises mainly help to fine-tune the technical aspects, but in addition the chapter constructs a link with understanding particular situations and with applications in an official competition (8-on-8 soccer). Training and competition are always viewed as a unit, one being tightly linked to the other. Game-oriented practice, found in this chapter, stimulates young players more than do instruction and training sessions (as are so frequently observed in other approaches to youth soccer) whose contents are isolated from the competition.

Taking Soccer Into the Future

"The soccer of the past we have to respect, the soccer of today we must study, and the soccer of the future we should anticipate."

Boran Milutinovic

Players should encounter training that is enjoyable, effective, and appropriate to their age as soon as they set foot on the field. This is the only way to develop healthy, happy, talented soccer players. Any attempt to rush the natural development of young soccer players or have them confront the demands of the full game too early has to be considered detrimental to their development and future performance.

Bringing the Game out of the Middle Ages

Neil Postman, a professor of sociology at the University of New York, states in his book *The Extinction of Childhood* (1992) that modern society often does not allow children to distinguish their mode of living from that of adults (reported in *La Vanguardia*, circa December 1993). "They are eating the same food, they are watching the same television program, commit crimes like adults, take alcohol at an early age as well as drugs." He further states, "The world of labor is also getting out of control. Girls between 12 and 17 years of age are, today, among the world's best-paid models, and there are children who, at the age of 18, are already multimillionaires (actors or pop stars). It is impossible that these children are behaving and will behave in the future as normal children would. . . ."

According to Postman, it's very dangerous when society does not notice much difference between the world of children and that of adults. He believes that children must discover the mysteries of life slowly and step by step, always in accordance with their mental stage and their present capacities.

The environment that children move and play in today has suffered an enormous transformation from nature to urban jungle. This development has denied children the chance to learn from and follow nature. Instead they are more often forced to move against their own nature (to cross the road only when there is a zebra path or play computer games instead of outdoor games in fresh air). Because children have lost the natural setting, which influenced the education and development of their parents and grandparents, they should be given modern surroundings for learning and gaining experience on their own that can replace the former ones. This is why having organized sports in schools and clubs is so important for the quality of life of our youth!

Our world of soccer reflects the current situation. Instead of children being able to practice their particular games, as in the past, in the streets or other natural settings, the increasing urbanization of the landscape does not allow most of them to make use of the natural surroundings that their grandparents had for play.

Besides having to play the game on artificial grass fields far away from their homes, in our advanced society young boys and girls—in many clubs and schools—must maintain rigid training methods and competitions. These old-fashioned methods in no way respect the laws of nature or the children's actual mental and physical capacities.

Everywhere children are obliged to train and compete like adults, forced to adapt to rules originally intended for adults. The rush to introduce talented youth to the adult game has frequently resulted in their acquiring bad habits that later limit their performance on our senior teams.

We know that when an institution organizes a competition, it determines to a high degree the objectives, contents, and methods of the children's training and learning process. That means that if the structure of the competition is wrong, the way the coach trains them must also be incorrect.

Children should take part in games that are specially designed for their age, rather than being rushed into the complex adult game.

Experience shows that coaches of young players are seen positively by the parents and club officials only when the kids demonstrate success or winning. But to achieve this kind of success in the traditional competition, the coaches must train them in a very similar way to the adults, with more or less the same contents and methods.

Beginners in such a system are obliged to compete every weekend in a match where success is conditioned mainly by one specific skill (the long pass) and often by destructive or negative tactics. This forces the coaches, in the limited available practice time (generally 3 hours a week), to concentrate almost exclusively on match-winning aspects. They are afraid to "waste time" in developing the children at the initial stage through a wide range of physical activities and problem-solving situations. But it is only in this systematic way that a sound level of coordination and conditioning capacities can be acquired. And these, as we all well know, are indispensable for the further improvement of young players' performance.

Although sport scientists agree on this developmental model, few sports federations are making use of the important recommendations these professionals make. Instead of copying nature and patiently developing all the necessary capacities, through training and competitions tailored to the children's capacities, many coaches of young players still force them to play like clones of an adult.

Modifying Postman's words slightly, we might affirm the statement: Once we give the children access to the forbidden fruit of adult information (competition), we expel them from the garden of infancy. It does seem as though, in many parts of the world, there are too many teachers and coaches of young soccer players still living in the Middle Ages. Why call it that? In the Middle Ages society knew only infants and adults. By six or seven years of age, a person was already considered adult because he participated in adult activities: the child worked, ate, dressed, and behaved as an adult.

For how long can we allow the ignorance of these coaches and administrators to continue to obstruct the natural development of the next generation of soccer players?

"The best advice I could give to young players is to make use of every minute and don't hide in a box that others have constructed for them."

Michael Jordan

Ten Rules for Continuous Improvement

1. Be prepared to give up your prior way of thinking.
2. When you teach, always question what and how you teach and what you have done up to now.
3. To overcome certain weaknesses and deficiencies of a player or a team, it is not enough to detect and diagnose the problems: you must seek their roots and apply the corresponding remedies.
4. To prepare a fine performance in the next match, consider and perfect every small component of the performance; small details may change the circumstances dramatically.
5. Progress step by step.
6. A 100 percent solution is difficult to find.
7. The difference between a good performance and an excellent one is putting in some more effort.
8. The best preparation for tomorrow is doing an optimal job today; the final victory results from a series of small, daily successes.
9. As none of us knows so much as all of us, working in a team ensures better results.
10. The process of continuous improvement never finishes.

You have a step-by-step program here, designed precisely to match young players and to nurture their motivation to grow and develop in the game. Through this developmental model, you can help them flourish, year by year, as better and better players on the way to the wonderful adult game. You can foster their love of sport and good soccer playing.

Measurement Conversions

Because of the international popularity of soccer, this text uses metric measurements throughout the text and artwork.

To convert meters to yards, consult the following conversion chart or multiply the number of meters by 1.093611. For example, 55 meters × 1.093611 = 60.148605 yards. Round to 60.2 yards. (Note: .1 yard equals about 3⅝ inches.)

Meters	Yards	Meters	Yards	Meters	Yards
1	1.1	26	28.4	51	55.8
2	2.2	27	29.5	52	56.9
3	3.3	28	30.6	53	58.0
4	4.4	29	31.7	54	59.1
5	5.5	30	32.8	55	60.2
6	6.6	31	33.9	56	61.2
7	7.7	32	35.0	57	62.3
8	8.8	33	36.1	58	63.4
9	9.8	34	37.2	59	64.5
10	10.9	35	38.3	60	65.6
11	12.0	36	39.4	61	66.7
12	13.1	37	40.5	62	67.8
13	14.2	38	41.6	63	68.9
14	15.3	39	42.7	64	70.0
15	16.4	40	43.7	65	71.1
16	17.5	41	44.8	66	72.2
17	18.6	42	45.9	67	73.3
18	19.7	43	47.0	68	74.4
19	20.8	44	48.1	69	75.5
20	21.9	45	49.2	70	76.6
21	23.0	46	50.3	71	77.7
22	24.1	47	51.4	72	78.7
23	25.2	48	52.5	73	79.8
24	26.3	49	53.6	74	80.9
25	27.3	50	54.7	75	82.0

Bibliography

Almond, L. 1983. "Teaching games through action research." Pp. 185-197 in *Teaching Team Sports*. Roma: Comitato Olimpico Nazionale Italianio/Scuola dello Sport.

Andresen, R., and G. Hagedorn. 1976. *Zur Sportspiel-Forschung*, Band 1. Berlin: Bartels und Wernitz.

Blázquez Sánchez, D. 1995. *La iniciación deportiva y el deporte escolar*. Barcelona: INDE Publicaciones.

Diem, C. Lectures author attended at Deutsche Sporthochschule Köln, 1960s.

Dietrich, K. 1968. *Fussball Spielgemäss lernen-spielgemäss üben*. Schorndorf (Germany): Verlag Hofmann.

Dietrich, K., and G. Landau. 1976. *Beiträge zur Didaktik der Sportspiele*, Teil 1. *Spiel in der Leibeserziehung*. Schorndorf (Germany): Verlag Hofmann.

Durand, M. 1988. *El niño y el deporte*. Barcelona: Ediciones Paidos.

Gallahue, D. 1973. *Teaching Physical Education in Elementary Schools*, 5th edition. Philadelphia: W.B. Saunders Company.

Gallahue, D., and B. MacClenaghan. 1985. Movimientos fundamentales: su desarrollo y rehabilitación. Buenos Aires: Ed. Médica Panamericana.

Gould, D., and M. Weiss, eds. 1987. *Advances in pediatric sport sciences*, vol. 2. Champaign, IL: Human Kinetics.

Halliwell, W. 1994. "The motivation in team sports," *Apuntes de Educación Física y Deportes*, no. 35 (Barcelona), 51–58.

Leitner, S. 1991. *So lernt Man lernen*. Freiburg (Germany): Herder Verlag.

Leitner, S. 1972. *So lernt Man lernen*. Freiburg (Germany): Herder Verlag.

Mahlo, F. 1981. *La acción táctica en el juego*. La Habana: Ed. Pueblo y Educacíon.

Martin, D. 1982. *Grundlagen der Trainingslehre*. Schorndorf (Germany): Verlag Hofmann.

Millmann, D. 1979. *The Warrior Athlete—Body, Mind, and Spirit*. Walpole, NH: Stillpoint Publishing.

Morehouse, L., and L. Gross. 1977. *Maximum Performance*. New York: Mayflower Granada Publishing.

Mosston, M. 1988. *La enseñanza de la educación física*. Buenos Aires: Ediciones Paidos.

Ostrander, S., N. Ostrander, and L. Schroeder. 1979. *Leichter lernen ohne Stress–Superlearning*. Bern: Scherz Verlag.

Pierce, W., and R. Stratton. 1981. "Perceived sources of stress in youth sport participants." In *Psychology of Motor Behavior and Sport*. Champaign, IL: Human Kinetics.

Robbins, A. 1987. *Poder sin limites*. Barcelona: Ediciones Grijalbo.

Spackmann, L. 1983. "Orientamenti practici per l'insegnamento dei giochi." In *L'insegnamento dei Giochi Sportivi*. Roma: CONI–Scuola dello Sport.

Thorpe, R., and D. Bunker. 1983. "A new approach to the teaching of games in physical education curriculum" In *Teaching Team Sports*. Roma: CONI - Scuola dello Sport.

Thorpe, R., D. Bunker, and L. Almond, Eds. 1988. *Rethinking games teaching*. Northans (England): Loughborough University.

Wahlsten, J., and T. Molley. 1995. *Quality ice hockey*, Vol. 2. of *Understanding and Learning the Game of Ice Hockey*. Helsinki: Finlands Ishockeyförbund.

Wein, H. 1999. *Fútbol a la medida del adolescente*. Sevilla: Federación Andaluza de Fútbol.

Whitmore, J. 1997. *Coaching for Performance*. London: Nicholas Brealey Pub.

Wilson, V. 1984. "Help children deal with stress factors found in competition." In *Momentum, Journal of Human Movement Studies*, Vol. 9, no. 1 (Edinburgh): 26–28.

Ziglar, Z. 1986. *Pasos hacia la cumbre del éxito*. Bogota: Editorial Norma S.A.

About the Author

Horst Wein is perhaps the world's foremost mentor of soccer coaches and trainers. He has coached the coaches of institutions in 51 countries covering four continents and has written 31 sports-related textbooks, including four on soccer.

Wein, an Olympic silver medal winner as a coach, was the first coach from the Western world to be invited to train top athletes in the former Soviet Union in the late 70s. He has also served as a consultant for two Olympic Games, the Asian Games, and for one of the most important soccer clubs in the world—Internazionale Milan.

Currently, Horst Wein works cooperatively with the Center for Research and Studies (CEDIF) of the Royal Spanish Soccer Federation. He also travels widely to adapt the game of soccer to better suit young players. Recently, Nike United Kingdom appointed him as head coach for their famous Premier Football Training Program. He resides near Barcelona, Spain.